The Healthy High

**HOW TO MANIFEST
AN ECSTATIC LIFE
WITHOUT BURNING OUT**

SHANNON~THE GOOD WITCH

The Healthy High

How to Manifest an Ecstatic Life Without Burning Out

Shannon Chavez

Copyright © 2024 Reflek Publishing
All Rights Reserved.

No part of this publication may be reproduced, distributed, or transmitted in any form or by any means, including photocopying, recording, or other electronic or mechanical methods, without the prior written permission of the publisher, except in the case of brief quotations embodied in critical reviews and certain other noncommercial uses permitted by copyright law.

Disclaimer: The author makes no guarantees concerning the level of success you may experience by following the advice and strategies contained in this book, and you accept the risk that results will differ for each individual. The purpose of this book is to educate, entertain, and inspire.

For more information: ShannonTheGoodWitch.com

ISBN Paperback: 978-1-962280-35-8
ISBN eBook: 978-1-962280-36-5

This book is dedicated to you and the magic you're making in the world!

Keep shining!

RESOURCES

You can find a growing list of resources and recommendations at ShannonTheGoodWitch.com/TheHealthyHigh including printable worksheets and videos to help you implement the lessons you'll learn within the pages of this book.

Enjoy!

THE GOOD WITCH MISSION

We believe all people are inherently valuable, worthy and deserving of the pursuit of a good life. We are passionate about helping humans create more utterly blissful moments in the everyday through coaching, community, books and digital products. $1 from every digital product is donated to getting resources to people in need. You can learn more about our mission at ShannonTheGoodWitch.com.

TABLE OF CONTENTS

Introduction: The Moonbeam Express 9
Welcome Poem: Shine Your Light 19

Part One: Breakdowns Lead to Breakthroughs 21
Chapter 1: In The Weeds 23
Chapter 2: I Picked You 33
Chapter 3: The Cost of Living 49
Chapter 4: Pivoting with Purpose 55
Chapter 5: Falling into Flow 71
Chapter 6: Opening Up 79
Chapter 7: Own Your Magic 89

Part Two: Harnessing Your Innate Power 101
Chapter 8: Thoughts Become Flesh 103
Chapter 9: You Are a Divine Creator 111
Chapter 10: Manifesting with the Moon 127
Chapter 11 : Celebrate Your Harvest with The Full Moon 137
Chapter 12 : Clear The Way for New
Growth with The Waning Moon 145
Chapter 13 : Connect to Your Divine Nature
with The New Moon 161
Chapter 14: Cultivate Your Dream Life with the Waxing Moon ... 171
Chapter 15: Manifesting Money 179
Conclusion: Before You Go 191
Farewell Poem: When the Spring Comes 197
Acknowledgements 199
Author Bio 203

INTRODUCTION
The Moonbeam Express

So you've heard all the hype around manifestation. I have a feeling you've got a good idea of what the term means, and maybe you've even seen it working in your life. Perhaps you believe in it, but you don't exactly understand it. It's a mystical concept—I totally get it. I've been studying the art of manifestation since 2007 and it still blows my mind!

Manifestation is a buzzword. It comes up in my coaching sessions and casual conversations with my peers almost daily. I've noticed that people can feel it. They know that they've got this **immense, powerful force at their fingertips, just waiting to be put** to good use, but because their minds can't fully grasp it, they're not practicing it with intention. They're still hustling toward their goals **because they haven't quite figured out how this whole manifestation thing works yet.**

If you're one of those people who knows they're powerful—who knows they're magic—please keep reading.

I promise that you don't have to comprehend all the ins and outs of manifestation to use it to your advantage. (You probably don't know how the internet works either, but that doesn't stop you from using it every day.)

You've likely got a list of milestones you want to reach in the foreseeable future. How can you make sure that you don't run out of gas before you reach your destination? At the end of your road trip, how can you be sure that all the time you spent in the car and all the money you spent on tolls and fuel will feel worthwhile? Did you enjoy the journey and catch all the sights along the way? What if you were so focused on your map that you missed the flashing lights the Universe was sending to direct you somewhere better?

Chasing dreams with reckless abandon is exhausting, so stop chasing and start attracting!

My purpose for this book is to help you manifest a life that feels as good as it looks.

As a purpose-driven action-taker with a deep desire to do good in the world, I've run myself empty a time or two in pursuit of my goals; but through trial and error, I've learned that it *is* possible to manifest an ecstatic life without burning out. There's a sustainable solution.

When I learned about the phases of the moon and what they symbolize in magical practices, it all clicked! As a living, breathing, human being, I'm a part of nature. Nature is cyclical; therefore, I am cyclical. I'm full of potential, but that doesn't mean I'm meant to be serving every hour of every day. It's important to carve out peaceful moments away from the hustle and bustle to rest and reset so that I can hear the voice of my intuition coming through. My growth depends on it!

Here's how I've come to think of it:

Life is a carnival. It's noisy. It's busy. There's stuff happening everywhere! You could be over here, watching a magic show or over there in the moon bounce. Maybe you're hanging out with the roadies behind the bleachers, getting drunk and smoking cigarettes. There are all these distractions.

So, imagine you're at the carnival and you realize you need a little break from all this commotion, and you think to yourself, "I'd love to go hop on the ferris wheel!" Maybe you're afraid of heights, so you're nervous, but you just want to have some fun and regroup. So, you ditch your buddies, grab some tokens, and hop on the ferris wheel.

As you start to make your way up, it's as if you're breaking free. While you're stopped at the top, it's quiet. The bird's eye view gives you a fresh perspective and helps you hear the voice of your intuition coming through. You're tuned in and you feel inspired! Suddenly, a lightbulb goes off! Maybe you're struck by a million-dollar idea, or you find yourself with the answer to a problem you've been trying to solve for weeks! You giggle with butterflies in your tummy as your cart begins to move again. You envision yourself going forward in your pursuits with this same steady sense of ease and enjoyment you're feeling as your cart circles back toward the ground with the momentum of gravity.

There's no resistance—it's effortless.

When the ride pauses at the bottom, you pop off with glee and run to tell your friends what you learned. You start to share your experience with everyone you meet. Imagine you take this sense of excitement into everything you do for the rest of your time at the carnival, and you connect with someone that shares your enthusiasm for life. So next time, maybe you ride the ferris wheel together and feel called to create something even more powerful than you could have imagined on your own because it all suddenly makes sense, and you finally have the help you needed to bring your vision to life!

Maybe you go on to create a club at the carnival and continue to attract more and more people who share your values. You're no longer overwhelmed and distracted by the madness. You're fulfilled by every experience. And now you know that if at any point you start to feel anxious or lost, you just hop on the ferris wheel to reset and reconnect to your highest self—the one who always knows what to do.

So, if life is like a carnival, "manifesting with the moon" is like riding the ferris wheel–maybe we call it the Moonbeam Express!

The simple, yet transformative manifestation ritual I've weaved throughout this memoir is inspired by the cyclical rhythms of nature. In Part Two: Harnessing Your Innate Power, I'll introduce the four primary phases of the lunar cycle and how you can work with them to create more ease and abundance in your life, but first, I'm pulling back the curtain on my personal odyssey down an overgrown path and all the teachable moments that led me here. In Part One: Breakdowns Lead to Breakthroughs, I'm vulnerably sharing my redemption story because I'm a prime example that change *is* possible.

If I can do the work, so can you!

Before we embark on this journey together, allow me to officially introduce myself. . .

I'm Shannon~The Good Witch and I'm honored to be your guide!

I tend to fumble when I try to sum up the hats I wear as a multi-dimensional human. All I really know for sure is that I'm made of magic, and so are you.

Introduction

I wrote *The Healthy High* because I felt called to tell you that **you matter beyond measure.**

We're all part of a miraculous, infinite substance that makes up the Universe.

We're teeny, tiny, subatomic *parts* of one gigantic *whole*.

On a soul level, there is no separation between us, but here on earth, your one-of-a-kind aura adds something special to the planet, and for that alone, you are worthy of an ecstatic life!

You don't have to be perfect to be a good person and you **certainly don't have to have it all figured out to make a positive impact in the lives of others.** Every good deed, every act of service, and each drop of kindness—no matter how big or how small—creates a ripple effect of positive change. Plus, it feels great to give back!

A little more about my entrepreneurial journey. . .
In the Spring of 2016, I quit my job as the morning anchor for a small town television news station in Bridgeport, West Virginia and returned to bartending at a local pub in my hometown of **Pittsburgh, Pennsylvania. That fall, I started my first business as** a wedding videographer and portrait photographer. In 2020, my husband and I purchased a second home that we transformed into **my photography studio and our first of two rental properties.** In the Spring of 2022, I enrolled in the Dharma Coaching Institute with a longing to help people on a deeper level and graduated that fall as a **certified Spiritual Life Coach and Dharma (Soul Purpose) Coach.** In 2023, I retired from weddings with a desire to create more space in my days for the work that lights me up. I've made it my mission to live my dharma, so that I can inspire the people I meet to live theirs.

Growing up, I felt like a jack of all trades, but a master of none. I just couldn't find that one thing that felt like it was meant for me. As a passionate achiever with the mindset that I could have, be, and do anything I wanted, I found myself drained and confused. Ambition, confidence, and a desire to do good in the world certainly served me well in life, but it wasn't until I got to the bottom of who I wanted to be that I started to manifest anything that felt significant.

When I left my career in broadcasting, people thought I was crazy; but I knew I was made for more. I used to think that I was indecisive, but now I see that I've just never been afraid to change my mind or own up to making a choice that no longer feels aligned. I'm learning, growing, and changing every day. It makes sense that my goals and dreams would grow and change too, right? Now when I'm setting goals, I loosen my grip to any specific destination, I look to my purpose as my North Star, and I act on aligned opportunities that present themselves along the way. I surrender to the journey because I trust beyond the shadow of a doubt that the Universe has—and always will—have my back.

Now, as a coach, I love using magic as a tool to help people think in grander terms for their lives. I love magic so much because the word "magic" alone feels expansive! It opens my mind to all that's possible. It feels big! It feels abundant! It feels effortless.

I was lucky enough to grow up in a household where magic was a regular topic of discussion. I loved spell books, TV shows, and movies about witches. My mom liked magic too and always said she was psychic. We'd play a game where I'd think of a number, and she'd have to guess it. She usually could! We never had much of a routine around magic or spirituality or anything for that matter. We

Introduction

went to church sporadically and I attended Sunday school, but when it came time for my confirmation, I got sick and couldn't make it. It never felt important enough for me to be confirmed, and maybe it was a blessing in disguise. I believed in God, and I liked going to church, but religion never really resonated with me.

I always felt powerful–like I could make things happen. I'd try to light candles by blowing on them like I'd seen Sandra Bullock do in the movie *Practical Magic* and my friends and I would play games like "Light as a Feather, Stiff as a Board," where we'd form a circle around someone laying on their backs and lift them up with the power of our minds, using only our fingertips.

My childhood was full of wonder, but I remember feeling frustrated by my spell books because I never had access to all the tools and ingredients listed out to perform a spell correctly.

When I was in eighth grade, my cousin CJ introduced me to the ideas of quantum physics and consciousness when he showed me the 2004 film *What the Bleep Do We Know*. The following year, I discovered the 2006 documentary, *The Secret,* and I was hooked on the idea that I could create my reality with my thoughts.

My friend Carter Redwood was the only kid my age that shared my interest in manifestation. When we weren't playing footsies in theater class, we were talking about *The Secret*. Carter was a talented actor. He knew that acting was his future. I always admired Carter's clarity and purpose. I thought, *If I only had something like that—one particular calling or talent—then I'd be able to manifest my dream life.*

When you have a definite purpose, you can manifest anything, but what if you don't have one definite purpose? Where do you focus your energy?

This is where I began to feel like a failure. I started to feel like a quitter. It took me thirty years to figure it out, but now I see that it's never going to be just one thing. I had to start looking at the bigger picture for how I wanted to *feel* and make tiny adjustments that brought me a little closer to that feeling! With each pivot, I got closer. Closer to something that felt satisfying.

Sometimes I felt like I had to take two steps backward before getting any further ahead. Sometimes I felt like I wasn't going anywhere at all, but I see now that it was all part of the plan—part of the lesson I was meant to learn and share.

It's been a dream of mine to publish this book for nearly a decade. Word's flow through me when I'm channeling my highest-self and I'm certainly *not* always my highest self, so I started writing to leave a trail of breadcrumbs to follow when I'm feeling lost.

Within these pages, I'll help you build a practice of grounding down and tuning in to your spiritual nature. This book is packed with anecdotes, acronyms and actionable steps I've gathered to aid you in your personal growth. Take what you will from the stories I'm about to share and look to this guide when you need a little direction. This isn't a road map. Think of it more like a tool kit. It might look small, but it's overflowing with useful resources.

So, without further ado, please grab your lantern and follow me into the weeds. Rest assured, there's sun on the other side of the shadows. You might get a little dirty, but I promise it's going to be worth it. Remember, this is your quest after all, so take your time and pause when you need a breather. I'll be here when you're ready to start again.

Let's dig in!

What are you looking forward to as you set forth on this journey? Take a beat to reflect on your initial thoughts and consider setting an intention to pause after each chapter to soak in what you learned.

WELCOME POEM:
Shine Your Light

You can do anything when you use your mind.

All you have to do is think about it all the time.

Think about it every night before you go to sleep,

and think about it when you wake and you're in for a treat.

Smile when you brush your hair and when you brush your teeth.

Dance around and sign this song, then hop into a seat.

Close your eyes and visualize what you want to see.

All you have to do is think about it and believe!

And one more thing, my dear Moonbeam, I should have said before:

Don't forget to turn the key and open every door!

Take your time, but don't get stuck waiting for a sign.

Hop on up and trust your gut to guide you all the time.

For in the stars you'll find a path to lead you through the trees.

They'll light the way to all that's good and show you prophecies.

And in the wind you'll hear a call, listen for its song.

Dance and sing and shine your light and you can do no wrong.

PART ONE:
Breakdowns Lead to Breakthroughs

CHAPTER 1
In The Weeds

If you've ever worked in the service industry, you probably know what it means to be "in the weeds." Maybe it's a Friday night and on top of your regular customers, you've got three birthday parties, a retirement celebration, and four separate kickball teams that piled in after their tournament. You're out of menus, trying to roll more silverware, taking orders, cashing out checks and bussing tables all at once and you've been trying not to pee your pants for the past ninety minutes. Even the very best and well-seasoned servers find themselves in the weeds from time to time. If you're lucky, you've got a team to rely on and you can simply tell your kitchen staff, "I'm in the weeds" so that they can start running food and you can tell your bartender, "I'm in the weeds" and they can start to hand off drinks to your tables while you run to the bathroom. Soon enough, with a little team effort, you're out of the weeds and back on track, hopefully taking home hundreds of dollars in tips for the hard work you put in that night. All you had to do was say, "I'm in the weeds" and suddenly, everyone started pitching in.

If only life was always that easy!

In my experience, life is full of weeds, but there's not a built-in team of people to take over when I need a breather or some manual to follow when I'm feeling overwhelmed. When I was stuck in the weeds in my own life, I didn't know how to ask for help and I certainly didn't have the systems in place to go missing in action while I gathered my bearings, so I did my best to keep things running on my own with no end in sight to the madness.

If you're anything like I used to be, you probably buzz around like a busy little worker bee, managing multiple projects at once. I bet you're so dedicated to showing up for those you love that you'll sacrifice your own well-being to get the job done. You have high expectations for yourself and struggle to loosen your grip on the reins of your responsibilities because you fear what might happen if you dare step away for a break. I have a feeling you don't like missing out or letting people down, so you use quick pick-me-ups like caffeine and carbs, a spontaneous shopping spree, or a night out partying with friends to keep you going. By the end of the day, you're so physically fatigued that even brushing your teeth and getting into bed feels like a struggle. You're constantly fighting the comedown, but you're convinced it's all worth it, so you adapt and find the pleasure in it. You've even secretly started to like the feeling you get in the pit of your stomach when you reach that highest peak, just before toppling over the hill at lightning speed toward the lowest valley. It drives you crazy, but you crave the thrill, so you keep lining up for the roller coaster.

If any of this is resonating with you, you're not alone. Trust me when I tell you that I know what you're going through. As a recovering perfectionist committed to being the best version of

Chapter 1

myself for the people around me, I struggle to let my guard down. It's always felt easier to share the bright and shiny sides of myself because lifting people's spirits brings me joy.

I'm a people pleaser with a passion for service.

Sometimes if feels like I'm carrying the weight of the world on my shoulders.

In a virtual room with four other women in the spring of 2021, my coach, Eva Lin, asked a powerful question that shook me to my core. When she asked,

"What would you do if you had six months left to live?"

I broke down in tears. It's not like me to get emotional around other people, but this question struck a chord. I thought of my friends and family. I wanted to call everyone and tell them I loved them!

I suddenly felt as if none of the stuff I'd been working on mattered.

Leading up to that point, I was excited for the new direction I was heading with my business after a year of working with coaches and taking every digital course that I could get my hands on during the pandemic. I created a content calendar and mapped out an entire year of podcast episodes, planning to re-launch the show and open the doors to a group coaching program by the fall.

Eva's question shifted something in me and left me feeling silly and selfish for exerting so much energy on my creative pursuits. After that call, I pushed my dreams to the side and devoted myself to being a better wife, a better daughter, and a better friend.

But before long, I teetered so far out of balance that I fell into a depression.

The Healthy High

By the end of a busy summer season in 2021, I was hanging on by a thread. As a newly married, 28-year-old woman with a loving partner, lots of friends, and multiple successful businesses, I looked ecstatic.

I'd filled my schedule so full of projects and obligations that I had no choice but to keep going and honestly, didn't even realize I was coming undone. I was blissfully unaware of the emotional turmoil brewing inside of me and how it was impacting the world around me. I ignored the signs and settled for temporary highs to get me through the days.

But on the inside, I was crumbling.

Eventually, the chaos happening in my inner world started showing up in my outer world. My work was piling up with no end in sight and I was having regular nightmares about drowning and being pummeled by mounds of sand. My body was trying to tell me that something was off.

I knew that if I wanted to get to the bottom of it, I'd have to ask for help.

I had an inkling that my friend Amy Walsh might want some new photos for her therapy practice, so I offered a trade, and she said yes.

I grabbed my camera, she grabbed her symbolic shovel, and we dug in.

In a matter of twenty minutes, Amy helped me see that my problem wasn't that I was burned out from my business or that I was hungover from drinking too much after a long day. It rooted deeper than that.

So, we kept digging.

Chapter 1

Why was I working myself to the bone? Why was I abusing drugs and alcohol? Was I running from something that felt too scary for my subconscious mind to face head on?

Turns out, I'd been collecting a ton of baggage and tossing it to the back of my closet.

In a Rapid Transformational Therapy session, we explored my habit of procrastination. I was taken to a memory of third grade.

I was wearing little red cowboy boots and a Power Puff Girl backpack. It was the day our report cards were handed out. I had a few Bs and a C so I was afraid to take it home to show my mom. I didn't want to get in trouble for failing to make straight As, so I held on to that report card as long as I could without showing her. I remember worrying and hoping that none of my friends would bring up that our grades were in, because I knew I'd be in even bigger trouble for hiding my report card, but the fear paralyzed me. I was ashamed of being imperfect and afraid of getting in trouble.

I don't remember the details about what came of my mom seeing my grades. I imagine she yelled—that was a pretty normal reaction for her—but it's not like she beat me or punished me in some outrageously traumatic way. It wasn't the end of the world, and it certainly wasn't a life-or-death situation, but my eight-year-old brain was terrified of what might happen. That was my first memory of procrastination and the beginning of a lifelong battle.

So, my habit of procrastinating then, must stem from a desire to be perfect. But why did I desire to be perfect?

The root cause was fear.

As human beings with thousands of years of generational trauma we've inherited through our ancestors, many of us suffer from the side effects of a deeply rooted instinctual fear of being alone. We're afraid of failure. We don't want to disappoint our friends and families. What if they stop loving us and leave? We're afraid to own up to our mistakes and tell our true stories because we don't want to let anyone down. This fear of being cast out of our tribes and left for the wolves creates a sense of urgency to fit in and prove our worth.

In my case, a desire to be valued and accepted led to perfectionism, perfectionism led to procrastination, procrastination led to overwhelm, overwhelm led to burnout, burnout led to depression, and depression led to more self-destructive habits like over-drinking and abusing drugs.

I'll share more about my breaking point a little deeper into this book, but for now, I'll summarize my healing journey since then:

After picking up the pieces of my crumbling identity, I began 2022 feeling mostly whole again. I enrolled in The Dharma Coaching Institute and got serious about becoming the highest version of myself so that I could become a better teacher. I built awareness around my habits and behaviors and focused on making small but mighty changes, taking things one day at a time and giving myself grace along the way. I learned to let go of things that weren't serving me, so that I could move forward with more ease and spaciousness for something better to come along in divine timing. I stepped out into the world as a fuller version of me, proud of who she is and what she wants. I invited people into my life that lift me up and encourage me to continue showing up as the highest version of myself.

Now, I embrace both the light and shadow sides of my soul and do my best to share my truth without fear of being misunderstood. Vulnerability has been the catalyst to my personal growth.

The more honest I can be about where I'm starting out, the easier it is to get to where I'm going.

Personal experience taught me that procrastinating only makes things worse. The longer I stayed stuck in my growing pile of despair, the harder it got to dig my way out.

It's like doing the laundry. When you're busy putting out fires everywhere else, you have an excuse to let your dirty clothes pile up, right? It's not a priority. It will get done eventually (or at least that's what you keep telling yourself anyway), but the thing is, no one else cares if your laundry goes through the wash. It's up to you to get it cleaned and pressed and neatly put away. Lucky for you, you don't have to do it alone. I like doing the laundry. I have a little song I sing when I'm doing my real-life laundry that makes the process more fun and I'm sure you can find it somewhere on my Instagram page, but for now, I'm here to help you sort through your symbolic laundry too. We'll take it one small load at a time. If you want less clutter and chaos in your outer world, tidy up your inner world. You're always going to have more laundry to do, so make it easier on yourself and find ways to enjoy it.

The teachings in this book are here to help you make the mess a little more magical.

If you're navigating a season of life that's overgrown with weeds, *celebrate* that you've got weeds in the first place. Weeds mean that the soil is fertile and with a little tender loving care, you can transform those weeds into a luscious garden.

God has plans for you. Everything you've been calling in wants to manifest in your life. In fact, it's already in progress. The Universe is simply waiting for you to make room for all the blessings it's sending your way.

If you want delicious fruits and vegetables, clear the weeds, turn the soil, plant the seeds and water them as they grow, but don't just do this once. Tend to your garden, year after year through every changing season and don't wait until you've got a perfect garden to enjoy your harvest. Among the weeds, you'll find wildflowers and four-leaf clovers. Keep your eyes peeled for the fruits of your labor hidden among the dandelions and celebrate even the dandelions because they give you an opportunity to wish for something different—something that will fill you up and sustain you as you do your life's work.

One by one, you'll pick the fruits of your labor and give thanks for your harvest. You'll reap the rewards all winter long as you rest and recharge. Come spring, you'll take what you learned from the year before and plant the seeds of only your favorite flowers and foods—the ones that flourished and brought you the most joy. And maybe the seeds that didn't succeed, you'll plant in a new place, and you'll water a little more and you'll continue the process over and over, finding more ease with every changing season.

You as a divine spirit in human form have everything you need to manifest an ecstatic life. The power lies within you. Whatever difficulties you're experiencing now might last a while, but they won't last forever and they're only preparing you for what's to come.

In the following pages, I'm sharing the very practices I've used to get out of the weeds for good! You'll learn to harness your

Chapter 1

innate spiritual power to manifest anything you could possibly desire without running out of steam or falling out of balance. You can expect to walk away from this book with a new appreciation of your unique circumstances and the confidence to blossom into the thriving being you were born to become!

The world deserves the highest version of you—How can you be the highest version of yourself for the people who need you if you're overwhelmed and burned out?

God wants you to feel ecstatic and fulfilled, but don't avoid the shadows. It's in the pain that you will find your purpose. You're going to have to climb your way out of whatever dark and scary hole you've been hiding in, but you don't have to do it alone. There's so much life waiting for you at the top, so let's get to it.

In Chapter Two: I Picked You, we're digging deeper than I thought I'd be brave enough to go in my first book, but I'd be remised if I tried to teach the lessons I've learned without sharing my full story. Join me on a trip down memory lane as we explore my deeply rooted unhealthy habits and the epiphany that helped me overcome my long and strenuous battle with burnout so that I could stop surviving and start thriving!

Before we jump in, pause for a moment of quiet reflection.

Can you pinpoint a time in your life when you were "in the weeds?" What was it like? How were you able to make your way out? Maybe you feel like you're in the weeds now. If that's the case, what are you experiencing? Reflect on your feelings and release them onto the pages of your journal.

CHAPTER 2
I Picked You

The power of positive thinking resonated with me as a young girl learning about manifestation, because I was a positive person by nature. Optimism was ingrained in me. I've always had a knack for being able to see the big picture and maintain a positive attitude—even in the hardest of times—trusting that it's all a part of a greater plan at work.

I was born into an environment where the wisdom of spiritual teachers and personal growth coaches like Deepak Chopra and Tony Robbins played on repeat. My mom wanted to create a happy life for us, so she was constantly working on herself. After six miscarriages, doctors told her that she would never be able to carry a child to full term, but despite the odds, she manifested me. When she held me for the first time on September 20, 1992, after more than twenty-four hours of natural labor and just shy of her forty-second birthday, she said I looked exactly as she pictured. Before I arrived, she painted a room pink and called it the nursery (or maybe it was my cousin CJ who would call it that) but either way, she prayed me into existence through creative visualization and persistence.

My mom's lifelong friend Tim, who's served as a role model and positive male figure in my life since birth, is another believer in magic and always reminds me that "I picked" my mom. When I was about three years old, I told a story with utmost certainty about being in heaven and choosing her from a screen where I was watching her vacuum the living room of my childhood home. I've always held a crystal-clear vision of this occurrence in my mind. I remember seeing her with long, curly, auburn colored hair and thinking, "She's the one." Whether or not this is a memory, a dream, or a story created by the mind of a toddler, I wholeheartedly believe that my soul chose my body, my birthday, and this exact human experience for a divine reason.

To me, being positive is about having hope in the unknown, believing whole heartedly that everything happening now is leading to my highest good and the highest good of all. But what if being so positive kept me from fully feeling?

Early on in life, I recognized that faith and forgiveness felt better than bitterness and resentment, so I suppressed my sadness and leaned into happiness. But what if there's more to life than being happy? Can I lead a full and peaceful life without the pain? I think I could do without the suffering, but not the pain. The good days wouldn't be so good if they were all good.

True magic lies in the contrast.

I was raised in what you'd call a "dysfunctional family." My dad drank a lot and prioritized fun over us, so my mom was basically on her own. Occasionally we'd get some money out of my dad when my mom would send me into the bar looking for him. He'd watch me now and then when she was in a pinch, but for the most part, it was just me and my mom. Thankfully, my mom had a really great job and moved her way up the ladder, but she struggled, sacrificed and worked her butt off to provide for us.

Even though my dad was absent a lot of the time, I was surrounded by love.

My Pap Pap—my mom's dad—was our rock. My Grandma suffered from Alzheimer's Disease and moved to a nursing home when her memory worsened, but I remember her being full of joy until the very end of her life. She was always smiling and telling stories from her golden days when we visited. My pap was kind and funny and watched me when I was home sick from school. If it happened to be a Wednesday, I'd get to tag along with him and my Uncle Rege for a trip to the grocery store and lunch at Eat'n Park. They always made me laugh.

When I was six, my mom's sister Karen passed away from breast cancer and her three boys (my cousin's, Nick, Matt and CJ) took turns living with us. Even though my mom did a good job of staying strong, I know she was devastated. She was grieving the loss of her sister, but she still had mouths to feed, so she kept climbing in her heels and lipstick, making it look easy to the outside world.

My cousins were more like brothers to me. They teased me and chased me around with plastic poop and shook the ferris wheel cart to scare me when we were stopped at the top at Conneaut Lake Park every summer. I can remember being in daycare and arguing with other girls that they were my brothers not my cousins. They'd withstood more heartbreak than I could have imagined as a kid, but we came from the same roots, and they were my family. Nick was the oldest and started having kids of his own while he was still a kid himself, so I was blessed with second cousins that I called my nieces and nephews and felt abundantly grateful to have so many wonderful people in my life.

When I was twelve, we experienced another major loss when my Pap passed away at the age of eighty-four. He lived a full and happy life, but his death caused a rift between my mom and her brother, who had addiction problems of his own, so I lost my Uncle too.

The following year, my dad had a falling out with his business partner and needed a place to stay, so my mom let him move in with us. They didn't have a romantic relationship; she just opened her heart and home. He was a talented handyman, so he spent a few years living in our basement, fixing up the attic, maintaining the pool in our backyard, and helping around the house while she went to work to pay the bills. Eventually, he got a job with my cousin Nick, who was also living with us at the time and started making enough money to chip in for groceries and utilities. I remember he even gave us Christmas gifts that year—cash that he'd tucked inside of an empty cigarette box and wrapped in aluminum foil.

It was an interesting experience—my estranged father moving back in at the start of my teen years—but I was used to our house having a revolving door.

Things were pretty "normal" for a while. My dad continued to help with chores and stayed sober a lot of the time. He was never the kind of alcoholic that needed to drink every day. He could go months without booze or a cigarette, but the minute he'd get his hands on a bottle of whiskey, he'd down it within a few hours. My friends called him "Houdini," but not for the way he could make a bottle of liquor disappear, but because of all the times he'd suddenly appear out of thin air from the dark, unfinished basement where he'd stay most of the day. He never said much, but he was always friendly. Occasionally he'd emerge to the first floor to make a few Dagwood sandwiches and watch TV. He could also make an entire cake disappear quicker than the whiskey! Have I mentioned that he was a five foot six, Hispanic man, weighing in at about 130 pounds? (I guess I inherited his fast metabolism along with a high tolerance for alcohol.)

Unfortunately, this bout of support from my dad didn't last long and after a while, he quit his job and went back to hiding out in the basement, chain smoking cigs, downing fifths of Black Velvet and fighting with my mom. My dad and I lived under the same roof for years, but he was more like a distant relative than a father. He was quiet and kept to himself most of the time. My mom would get angry with me for being too nice to him, so I avoided conversations all together. They triggered each other and I was stuck in the middle. So even though I felt sad for him and didn't want to pick sides, it was clear I had to be on Team Mom.

I walked on eggshells through my entire adolescence, often feeling like I was the only adult in the room. A minor disagreement with my mom would throw her into a temper tantrum that could last an entire day of screaming and name calling, even when my friends were around. She didn't have a problem expressing her feelings. My quieter and more passive aggressive dad would eventually crack and call her a "fat cock sucker" or something absurd that would usually make us laugh. His go-to response to one of her reactive comebacks was "blow me."

My household was unbearable at times. I remember dreaming of the day that I would finally get the nerve to run away and start my own life in a far-off land, but I'd quickly forgive and forget those fantasies. When I "hurt my mom's feelings," setting off a rampage of hateful digs and crazed reactions, I'd make her a card to apologize, and she'd go right back to being a fun-loving mom until the next time I did something to upset her. I loved my mom more than anything and understood that she had a lot of unresolved trauma. She never learned to process her emotions in a healthy way. I wanted to help her see how great she was doing, but she had confidence issues and craved external validation, so I tried to comfort her with my company and words of affirmation. When I was on my best behavior, she was a kind and generous mother, so I learned to filter every single word that came out of my mouth. It wasn't safe to share my thoughts—that got me in trouble—so I became a people pleaser. I got good at hiding my emotions and doing my best to keep the peace.

As I grew older, however, I lost control of my tongue and started to speak up, only adding to the toxic energy in our household. The verbal abuse continued for more than a decade, and all the while, my relationship with alcohol and sex only grew stronger and more deeply woven into the fabric of my life.

By the age of fourteen, I was drinking with the neighborhood kids and consuming way more booze than a ninety-two-pound girl should be able to handle without puking. It didn't matter that I'd seen the ruin alcoholism and addiction could cause in families. Binge drinking and blacking out was normal and expected; it was in the circles I was running around with, anyway. I was surrounded by people who loved to drink and hook up. It was our common ground. It's what we did together. It was fun and easy and socially acceptable, especially when I went off to college.

Chapter 2

Getting drunk and having sex was a temporary escape from reality with people who just didn't really give a shit about what might happen. We had a mutual agreement that this was a safe place to get wasted. All that mattered was that we had the most fun possible, despite whatever was on the agenda for the upcoming day. We were risking everything but after one drink, none of it mattered. A "fuck it" kind of attitude took over and all my worries went out the window. I felt invincible and like I could finally let loose and express myself. Consequences didn't matter. Drinking made me feel brave and gave me permission to experiment. I could try anything! I could act on my desires with reckless abandon, knowing that I could always blame the booze if something went wrong. It didn't matter that I'd feel like crap the next day. I couldn't have cared less.

I wasn't doing this consciously—it was a part of my ritual. It's what we did. With every drink, I'd get a little hit of dopamine and with every sip, I'd lose a little more self-control.

By the start of 2021, my life was playing out like a telenovela.

Covid was on the rise again and there wasn't much to do in the world, so we drank, and not just a glass of wine or two. My husband, Alex, and I were blacking out at our basement bar, hosting friends until the early hours of the morning, and dancing to the same old songs. On one of those nights, I kissed my neighbor. Alex was right upstairs when it happened and I wish I could say it was just a sloppy drunk kiss, but the problem was, I was head over heels for this guy. He was a friend of Alex's from college who we'd bumped into at a brewery in the Summer of 2018. The instant I locked eyes with him, I knew I was in deep trouble, but I chalked it up to a crush and went on with my life.

Long story short, my harmless crush turned into an unhealthy obsession and after two and a half years of hiding my feelings from the entire world, I finally took a risk and told my love interest how I felt during a reckless night of binge drinking and began a short-lived secret relationship that would only lead to heartbreak.

But I think that somehow, expressing my feelings after biting my tongue for so long, cleared a blockage in my throat chakra. Suddenly, I was sharing my inspired ideas on Instagram every week and recording new podcast episodes. I'd come up with this eight-step goal setting process and decided that it was my ticket into the coaching space and out of dealing with the situation.

I was heading into 2021 with twenty weddings coming up—half of them rescheduled from the year before and slapped into my calendar—but rather than getting the back end of my business up in tip top shape, so that I wouldn't burnout again, I spent my days and nights pouring into this new project. I created an email funnel (a way to get people to subscribe to my newsletter) and planned to turn the process into a downloadable guide and an eight-week program that I'd host online for groups.

Can you tell I have an all or nothing kind of attitude? I can get really fired up and completely sucked into a new project or idea. I think my drive and tendency to hyperfocus is a form of procrastination. Like the drinking, it's another way my subconscious mind is protecting me from feeling all the feelings it would rather not deal with, because it doesn't feel safe.

Months passed and I still hadn't processed the romantic feelings I was having for someone that wasn't my husband. All those problems that I was avoiding were still there, hanging over my head,

Chapter 2

but now I was dizzy and drained from running in circles. I still hadn't spilled the tea about my scandal to anyone. Not a friend, not a coach, and not even my therapist. I thought I could keep it all in without dealing with it.

Time went on and life kept me busy. Alex and I modeled for photoshoots ahead of our upcoming nuptials and on the outside, looked like the same happy couple we'd always been. But the drinking continued. We threw parties for our friends, and even hosted my mom and her two cats for ten days after a carbon monoxide leak at her house. When her furnace was fixed and she was able to go home, she only took her cat Buddy and left sweet Julie behind because the cats didn't get along well, so we had this new responsibility of owning a pet and another gigantic distraction.

This sudden sense of urgency to show up for everyone else caused me to put my creative endeavors on hold. I didn't want to let anyone down, so I stopped doing things to fill my own cup.

Soon enough, our wedding came along smack dab in the middle of my busy shooting season. We partied hard on the big day and throughout the entirety of our honeymoon road trip through New England. We certainly had fun, but by the end of August, I wasn't just drained and hungover—I was depressed.

I've never thought of myself as a thrill seeker. You won't catch me skydiving or bungee jumping anytime soon, but this work hard, play hard kind of lifestyle gave me an adrenaline rush. I was addicted to the dopamine release that came from the anticipation of something exhilarating happening in my outer world. I'd do anything for a quick fix—a temporary high to satisfy some kind of nagging void inside of me. You know that pins and needles feeling when your leg falls asleep? How even though it's numb, it kind of stings. A weird concept of thinking that *not* feeling can be painful, but either way, it was like that. There wasn't a physical pain I could describe; it was more of an absence if that makes sense. An anomaly. So, I started searching high and low to quench my thirst for something I just couldn't put my finger on. I kept up my appearances, filling the cavity with distractions.

By this point, it was late September. There was a growing distance between Alex and I, and I could sense that my negative energy was rubbing off on him. A month after our wedding, he got fired from his job. He didn't want to tell his parents about it, just like he didn't want to tell his parents that he'd been fired from his first job years earlier, and he didn't want to tell them that we signed our marriage license two years before our wedding day. Like me, Alex is a people pleaser and fears disappointing people he cares about.

All these secrets triggered me because I was keeping the biggest secret of my own.

I'd lost my zest for life because I wasn't being myself.

One day, I remember waking up and feeling suddenly as if I'd been living in a play. Like I'd outgrown my life. I felt like I'd been wearing a mask for so long that I forgotten who I was. I coasted by, pleasantly unaware of my lack of fulfillment. I'd convinced myself that everything in my life was okay and continued to blame the burnout and binge drinking for my so called "funk."

I'd just gotten home from moving my best friend, Cody out to Colorado. We'd spent twenty hours alone in the car together, and I tried to tell him what was going on with me—why I wasn't my usual, happy-go-lucky self—but there was a frog in my throat. My tongue swelled every time I considered speaking the words of my affair.

Chapter 2

I didn't know how to express what I was feeling. I couldn't even comprehend it, and I think I felt like, if Alex didn't know, then no one else deserved to know either.

Somehow, I'd finally mustered up the courage to share my feelings with my therapist and by the end of our session, I knew that if I wanted to heal and move forward, I'd have to be honest with Alex. He was used to me getting cozy with girls at parties and being invited to bed. Threesomes kept our sex life spicy. We trusted each other and loved that we could be so open. So, why did this have to be any different?

The following day, a tragic loss cracked me wide open and all the emotions I'd been bottling up, poured out.

It was 7:30 p.m. on Tuesday, September 28, 2021, when we heard a knock at the door. Alex and I had just sat down at the kitchen table for dinner. Our neighbors from a block over were out walking their dog when they found our cat, Julie, lying unconscious in the front yard. My instincts took over and I ran to her side. She was warm, but she wasn't breathing, so I picked her up, Alex grabbed the keys, and we drove off to the closest emergency vet, praying and singing Rock a Bye Baby the entire way. We ran through the door, handed her over, and gave the medics permission to perform CPR, but it was too late. They believe she'd been hit by a car and died on impact from the trauma.

We brought Julie home in a box that evening with a few mementos like her pawprints molded into a clay ornament and a little vessel filled with a tuft of her speckled fur. Tears flooded from our eyes as Alex dug a grave in the backyard. We laid our sweet Julie girl to rest that evening with parts of ourselves that we'd been hiding.

Little did I know, this heart wrenching experience—the ending of a life—would be the beginning of my own transformation.

The floodgates opened and the release helped me to surrender. All the unprocessed pain came up at once and somehow, left me feeling better. But most importantly, it showed me that life without Alex would be impossible. How could I have done this without him? I believed in that moment that Julie gave up her life to bring us back together.

I loved Alex and I was ready to come clean. I wasn't sure what would come of telling the truth, but I knew that I couldn't continue hiding this huge piece of my heart. So, I wrote Alex a letter, printed it, and sealed it in an envelope.

All my life, I've struggled to express myself through spoken word. When I was little and wanted to make amends with my mom after a fight, I'd make her a card to say I was sorry. It was the easiest way for me to get my message across without fear of interruption or saying the wrong thing. I knew that if I wrote a letter, I had a better chance at being well received. I could write from the heart instead of speaking from my mind.

I was nervous about giving Alex my letter but felt a sense of relief knowing that everything I wanted to say was already out. There was no turning back. No changing my mind. All I could do now was trust that he would understand.

When I arrived home after leaving my letter for Alex to find, we sat quietly on the couch together, not knowing exactly where to begin. I told him I was sorry, and he said, "It's okay."

To my surprise, I was angry with his response. I guess I was hoping to get more out of him, so to see him so calm and reasonable triggered some pent-up feelings that I didn't even realize were there. I was depressed, I was numb, and what I certainly didn't need was more complacency.

I think part of me believed Alex wasn't going to be surprised at the news of my feelings for his friend. I thought he'd know exactly who I was referencing in my letter, but he didn't. He said he had absolutely no idea that any of this had been happening. I knew then, that we'd grown farther apart than I realized.

Did the fact that we never fought, that we never got angry, that we never got emotional mean that the spark between us had faded? I wondered if maybe there had never been a spark in the first place. Maybe there was no flame; just flammable material drowned in alcohol, ready to blow at any moment.

Suddenly, I wasn't sure we were going to be able to make it through this.

It all hit me like a ton of bricks. I wasn't his priority. I wasn't anyone's priority, yet I'd spent all this time hiding because I was afraid of hurting people.

Until that point, I'd been carrying all the blame for our deteriorating relationship, but it opened my eyes to the reasons that I'd fallen in love with someone else in the first place. We'd completely stopped spending quality time together. When we were out with our friends, he was so concerned with being "The Party Package" that he didn't even notice when I was absent.

Within moments, my anger subsided, and my walls went back up. I completely dissociated. I think that's when Alex realized how serious I was about changing my life, and that I was going to do it whether or not he was ready to come along for the ride. I was prepared to move forward without him if that meant getting my spark back.

But this epiphany moment saved our marriage. This explosion of emotions and uncomfortable conversation was exactly what we needed to jump start our recovery.

This was the turning point.

We realized that we had some serious work to do in our relationship, but most importantly, work to do on ourselves.

This is where we finally crossed over from going through the motions to living with intention.

I've rediscovered myself since then, and feel better than ever, accepting where I am and trusting that I'm on the right path. I see now that any struggle I experience or obstacle I face is God's way of guiding and strengthening me. I've found that creativity comes from vulnerability and art emerges from pain, but only when I know how to focus my energy. Now that I've learned to lean into my cyclical nature, honor my human emotions, and trust my intuition again, life feels easier and more magical!

There's no resistance.

During my dark night of the soul, I wondered what life might be like without alcohol, but it took another year and a half of arguing with myself before I finally made the decision to quit drinking. I decided that I no longer wanted to be an alcoholic who was "trying to cut back," but a person who simply "doesn't drink." That shift in my identity gave me the power to break the habit, so at thirty years old, I took the necessary steps to transform my routine.[1]

---

1. If you're curious about breaking some old habits and creating new ones, check out the best-selling book *Atomic Habits* by James Clear or simply visit ShannonTheGoodWitch.com/TheHealthyHigh for a complete list of supporting resources.

Chapter 2

Strict rules often leave me feeling trapped and uninspired, but I find that it helps to build awareness around my actions so that I can interrupt patterns that aren't serving me and create new ones.

To heal and make space for everything that's important to me, I had to ditch my "all or nothing" attitude.

"Everything in moderation," seems to be working better for me these days!

Once I changed my environment and filled my schedule with meaningful activities and worthy causes, it became easy to say no to drinks and now, I have a completely new relationship with alcohol that gives me permission to sip a tasty craft beer at a brewery or toast with a flute of champagne when there's something to celebrate, but I honor my limits and know when to quit.

I still go to parties, I still smoke weed most days, but now that I don't get drunk, I don't smoke cigarettes or rail lines of cocaine because I only did that when I was drunk.

My spiritual awakening got me thinking about all the reasons I stayed stuck for so many years in an unhealthy lifestyle. I thought about all the people in my life who were suffering through addiction and wondered what was keeping them stuck in their solace.

I'll share more of the lessons I learned on my road to recovery soon, but first, let's circle back to my parents. Why did they stay stuck in a hopeless marriage for twenty-five years?

Well, my mom had heard horror stories about the justice system and never wanted to worry about the potential of having to pay alimony to my dad who couldn't hold a steady job, so she settled for a less than magical life. She got used to his help with garbage night and groceries and traded her emotional well-being for his services.

My dad didn't like answering to my mom or being dependent on her money, but he was comfortable, so he stuck around.

Eventually, I convinced my mom that she deserved better—that they both did—and I helped them file for divorce. When they went their separate ways and moved into their own apartments, everything improved. They were happy and free to live independently on their own terms and I was finally able to create healthier relationships with each of them.

But what took them so long to get out of that terrible rut? Why did they wait so many years to move on? Before I attempt to name the problem, I'll share one more enlightening example of stuckness from my personal experience in Chapter Three: The Cost of Living.

I promise, there's a message in my mess and my only intention in sharing these intimate details is to help you see that anything is possible for you, no matter who you are or where you're starting out.

We can't flourish until we heal and sometimes, we have to crash and burn before we can rise from the ashes.[2]

It's all divine!

Take a moment to think about all that's had to happen to lead you to this moment. What have you overcome? Can you see the red thread that connects the dots?

CHAPTER 3

The Cost of Living

Before the world shut down at the start of 2020, I had $42,000 in my bank account—the most I'd ever saved up! When I started dating Alex, back in 2014, I had $99 to my name with pending bills and looming student loan debt. But I never let my lack of sufficient funds stop me from buying rounds of drinks at the bar for my friends every weekend, picking up a bag of blow for the squad, or giving a few bucks to panhandlers. I made money so that I could spend it and share it.

My mom taught me to be generous, so I was. She believed that money would always be available when we needed it, so she never worried about saving and always showed me to freely give to people in need. This mindset served me well in life in lots of ways, but I never learned how to manage my finances.

Alex comes from a "Leave it To Beaver" kind of family. He learned from his mom that "If you watch your pennies, your dollars will watch themselves," and started saving at ten-years-old. He went on to study Accounting at Duquesne University while I was there studying Broadcast Journalism. Besides a short dance together on the beach in Mexico during our senior year spring break, we hadn't crossed paths in our four years on the same campus. After graduation, Alex moved in with Jeremy Ehrlich, a good friend of mine from school who I'll tell you more about in Chapter Five: Falling into Flow. One morning while I was in Pittsburgh for the weekend during my two-year stint as a local news anchor in West Virginia, I invited Alex to tag along with Jeremy and me to brunch.

We hit it off and the rest was history.

Alex was smart and self-assured. I liked that about him. On our first official date, he helped me create a budget and up my cashflow by $150 per week with some savvy suggestions. I started to see how great it could feel to nurture my finances. At the beginning of our relationship though, I thought he was silly for "worrying" about money. I may have even criticized him for "being cheap" when he'd calculate his fifteen percent tip down to the exact penny. I'd always tip at least ten bucks at a restaurant, no matter the size of the check and even if it were all the money I had left.

Since then, we've learned from one another and adopted some new and more balanced principles. We both have an abundance mindset, while being money conscious. I see now that yes, although money is energy and energy must flow to grow, it also likes to feel safe and secure. If I didn't just want money to come to me, but I wanted it to stick, I would have to take care of it.

Money gives me the ability to live freely and passionately. When I'm stressed about paying my bills on time, I'm not able to experience the bliss of life.

My mom was carefree, but her lack of concern for the wellbeing of the money that she did have caused stress in other ways. She'd forget to pay the electric bill, so we'd come home to no power and be forced to get a motel room for the night. She'd forget to pay the cable bill, so I'd have to call in and pay the balance and a late fee over the phone with her debit card to get it switched back on. She was a hard worker and made a good living. We had a beautiful home and more than enough to get by, even without the support of my dad, but she was on her own and had trouble staying on top of her household responsibilities. She had bigger fish to fry.

Still, to this day, she usually has cash falling out of her purse and getting lost in the couch cushions. My lifelong friend, Rosa, and I used to dig through the furniture and my mom's old purses to find enough change to take the bus to the movies. We'd usually gather enough to stop at Taco Bell and pick up some food to sneak into the theater. This was a fun game for us, and we weren't being sneaky—just resourceful! My mom would have happily given us money for lunch and a show. She loved treating my friends and me to pizza and shopping dates. It was a constant party at our house. Every night was a sleepover with no bedtime and no rules. It was a blast, but obviously lacked structure.

After leaving my bartending job and going all in on my production company in 2018, I quickly saved up $42,000 from all the money I was raking in from shooting weddings. I appreciated the freedom that money gave me to travel, take my mom on vacations, and pay for lunches and lattes for my friends. Donating to the charities I always wanted to support and being able to invest in myself and things I believed in gave me confidence! I took pride in the success and abundance I'd been able to create as an entrepreneur and learned to celebrate my money more than I ever had before.

Every new booking meant another thousand bucks or so in my account, so even when I was feeling overwhelmed and overworked and started questioning whether I wanted to stay in the wedding industry, I continued sending contracts and taking those deposits. It took three and a half more years and many sleepless nights until I'd finally retire from weddings. Even though I'd grown up with an abundance mindset and never really feared going broke, I allowed myself to continue piling on commitments that felt stressful because the money made me comfortable.

I knew there would be plenty of other ways to make money. In fact, I said for years that I wanted to write a book. I wanted to teach people what I was learning about life and manifestation, and I knew that I wanted to be an author. I even saw the vision for publishing a best-selling book that would go on to make me millions of dollars that I could use to help people, yet I stayed trapped in my business, running in the same old circles for years until I finally decided that I would no longer stand for trading my time for money.

So, why did I do this to myself? Why did I stay stuck in my comfortable circumstances, despite a deep knowing that I was meant for more. Why did I procrastinate? Why did I drink too much? Why did I set my hopes and dreams to the side and continue letting the same old patterns play out?

I've come to the conclusion that my subconscious mind was trying to protect me. Even though I wasn't dying, I'd been programmed by years of generational trauma from my ancestors who were probably faced with life-or-death situations on a regular basis.

When I made the decision that I didn't just want to keep surviving, but I wanted to thrive, I started clearing the weeds and planting the seeds of my greatest intentions.

In Chapter Four: Pivoting with Purpose, I'm painting the picture of my soul-sucking career in television news and the misery that led to my entrepreneurial endeavors. Read to the end of the chapter for my take on goals and how you can set the kind that are worth pursuing.

CHAPTER 4
Pivoting with Purpose

I was two years out of college, $52,000 deep in student loan debt, 6,000 hours into my broadcasting career with no benefits, no vacation days, and at my wits end when I'd finally built up the courage to abandon the news industry and pursue something different—something fulfilling...

It was the spring of 2016 and I didn't know what I'd do next, but I knew that I couldn't waste any more time feeling so miserable.

A little context...

A couple of months before my college graduation, I was offered a position as the morning anchor and reporter for a small-town TV news station in Bridgeport, West Virginia. I hadn't applied for any jobs yet—this opportunity was handed to me on a silver platter—and even though I desired to go into sports or entertainment, I accepted the measly $22,500 salary they were dishing out and signed a two year contract.

I always loved design and transformation shows like *Trading Spaces and Queer Eye For the Straight Guy*. I thought it would be neat to help people feel more confident like Clinton Kelly and Stacey London were doing on *What Not To Wear* through head to toe fashion makeovers. I imagined having my own talk show like my idols Kelly Ripa, Oprah Winfrey, and Rachel Ray. I wanted to reach people around the world with a positive message! In highschool, I enjoyed taking photos and piecing together home videos in iMovie and thought maybe someday I'd produce box office trailers like Cameron Diaz's character in *The Holiday*, but when it came time to choose a college major, I landed on Broadcast Journalism because it made the most logical sense for a career in TV.

I'd worked my butt off through my four years at Duquesne building a resumé reel and growing my network through internships with the Pittsburgh Penguins NHL Hockey Team, *Pittsburgh Today Live* and the university's Athletic Department, but I guess I settled for a job in local news because the people around me said it would be "good experience." I'd been told by several mentors that if I wanted to be successful in television that I'd have to pay my dues and work my way up.

A few weeks after graduation in the Summer of 2014, I packed my bags and moved one hundred miles south of my hometown into an apartment with a fellow Duquesne grad who'd accepted a job at the same station as a daytime reporter. News was his passion and his excitement rubbed off on me, plus I was looking forward to the on-air experience and ready to make the most of it, so that's what I did. I put my best foot forward, as I had done with everything else in my life up until that point, and planned to squeeze every drop of good I could out of this learning opportunity.

Chapter 4

I never thought it would be easy, but I did think it would be worth it. Boy, was I in for a shock.

I was on the "early morning shift" from 12:00 a.m. to 10:00 a.m. Waking up before most people were even laying down for bed at night was grim. I'd arrive at the station at midnight to relieve the evening news staff. Someone always had to be there listening to the police scanner in case anything "newsworthy" happened, like an armed robbery or a deadly shooting. When the sirens went off, I'd have to book it to a news car with a camera and hunt down the scene of the crime while first responders were there for questioning.

Having a license was a requirement for the position, so I buckled down and passed my driver's test on the fourth attempt, just a few days before my move. Driving was still new and stressful enough during daylight hours, let alone in the middle of the night in bum-fuck nowhere where cell service was non-existent, and I needed to print out MapQuest directions to navigate the dark and scary dirt roads. Less than a month in, I drove a news car into a ditch at the scene of a fire. Luckily the police were nearby and kept a sense of humor as they pulled me out and flirted with me.

After these overnight adventures around "Wild and Wonderful" West Virginia, I'd rush back to edit the footage I captured in time for the show. At 5:00 a.m., frantically fix my hair and throw on some makeup as the show scripts printed so that I could pass them off to the control room guys, who thankfully, had my back! At 5:28 a.m., I'd sit behind the news desk as Keith counted us down to the show. Keith doubled as our camera operator and janitor. He was sweet and often brought me chocolate, but he was messy and sometimes had trouble holding on to his trousers. One day, his pants literally fell to the floor five seconds before we went live, and it took some serious self-control not to burst out laughing. That's what made me sad about the news. It was serious and solemn. Dramatic and depressing. At least when I went over to share something on the radio, we could relax and laugh on-air, but it was hardly that way at the news desk.

Thank goodness, I'd made a handful of good friends at work and was adopted by a local family who needed a babysitter for their precious little girls. If it hadn't been for them, I'm not sure I could have held on as long as I did. I justified my misery, because it wasn't all bad. I was gaining on-air experience right out of college and had done what I'd set out to do. I was learning the ins and outs of live broadcasting and still saw the job as a steppingstone to bigger and better things, so I stuck it out.

The constant levels of cortisol overload took a toll on my mindset and health. Before long, I found myself physically, mentally and emotionally drained from my work. I was regularly burdened by cold sore outbreaks and acid reflux flare ups. I felt utterly exhausted. It turns out, being a local celebrity with free dry cleaning and complementary gym membership with an unlimited tanning bed wasn't as glamorous as it was cracked up to be. I was broke, sleep deprived, sick to my stomach and far from the best version of myself.

Pittsburgh was only two hours away, so every single weekend, I'd drive straight home Friday afternoon after working all night and stay up until 4:00 a.m. partying with my friends. It took everything in my body to leave Alex on Sunday nights. I'd feel nauseated all day, and it wasn't just the hangover. It was dread. I'd wait until the very last minute to make the two-hour trek, usually getting back to my apartment with just enough time to shower and head into work at midnight on a total of maybe twelve hours of alcohol induced sleep since the Thursday before.

Chapter 4

I think I'm still catching up on all the sleep I missed out on during that two-year period.

I'd developed some unhealthy habits to get me through the nights. I'd keep an entire pot of coffee on my desk so that I could keep refilling my cup. I started smoking American Spirits and convinced myself they weren't that bad for me because they were "all natural" cigarettes. I'd take my friend's prescription Adderall pills any chance I could get my hands on them. I considered snorting lines of cocaine at work, but always saved it for the weekends. I'd guzzle an entire bottle of three-dollar wine or a few tablespoons of nighttime cold medicine to help me sleep during the day and carried over-the-counter pain meds and heartburn tablets with me everywhere I went.

About a year into the gig, my co-anchor left for maternity leave. The station was too cheap to bring on a substitute to take her place, so instead, I took over her responsibilities. I'd already been filling five positions as the anchor and reporter who'd shoot my own stories, edit my own videos and run my own teleprompter. Now I was also responsible for producing the entire ninety-minute morning newscast, plus *WV Midday*, the thirty-minute afternoon update. My ten-hour shifts extended to thirteen hours, five days a week for six months and I was forced to give up my beloved babysitting gig.

Interestingly, that six-month period was peaceful in comparison to my first year on the job. My co-anchor wasn't very fun to be around. Looking back, I can see she was going through a tough time, but her negative attitude weighed heavily on me. The tension in our space only added to the stress I was already feeling as a brand-new anchor with a million and one tasks to manage to make the show happen. While she was gone, I was finally able to find my voice and step into my role with a new sense of freedom.

In those six months, my confidence grew exponentially, and I started to recognize my value.

When she eventually decided that she wasn't coming back after her maternity leave, they opened her position. I was the obvious candidate for the job, and it was mine if I wanted it; but I really did not want to sign another two-year contract. I was considering it, however, so when it came time for my meeting with the higher ups to discuss the new salary and such, I asked for $30,000 per year. I'd just worked an extra ten hours per week for six months straight with zero compensation, so it was the least they could do for me, but instead, they laughed in my face and hired my roommate at $29,000.

I had never felt so undervalued in my entire life and suddenly realized just how replaceable I was in this industry. It was cutthroat, competitive, and demeaning in so many ways.

I thanked God I didn't settle.

I can hardly believe I lasted another few months there. I was under contract, so my only way out before June 2016 was to pay some ridiculous fee to terminate the terms early or bow out of broadcasting all together. I'd been scraping by as it was and collecting interest on my student loan payments. If it weren't for the money I was making in illicit side-hustles during my weekends partying in Pittsburgh, I would have had a hard time putting food on the table.

But eventually, I did find the courage to walk away. This life wasn't mine and I was tired of keeping up the charade.

One morning, my boss strolled in around 9:30 a.m. and something came over me. Heart pounding, I stood up, took a deep

Chapter 4

breath and walked over to his office. The moment I handed in my two weeks, a weight lifted from my shoulders.

I was free!

Just a few weeks before I finally cracked and quit, Joanna from *Animal Friends* brought in a beautiful tortoiseshell cat with the sweetest meow and a tongue like sandpaper that licked my hands through the entire two-minute segment on *WV Midday*. Her name was Julie and she'd been at the shelter for an entire year, the longest of any cat they had. She looked just like "Mummy Cat," a stray we took in when I was in high school during a giant snowstorm. After the show, I called my mom who I knew would be watching. We were on the same wavelength and agreed to adopt her! So that Friday, I picked her up, packed her in my Honda Civic and drove her to my mom's as I prepared to move home.

Although the going was tough, there were so many teachable moments and a whole lot of good that came from those two years in West Virginia. I certainly wouldn't be who I am today if I hadn't gone through the trenches.

I share the story of my newscasting journey because I want you to know that if you're feeling trapped or unsatisfied in your career, you have the power to make a change at any moment.

My exit from the news industry was a major turning point in my life, but it wouldn't be the last time I'd experience that feeling of complete and utter burnout. It was just the beginning of my long term, dysfunctional relationship with overworking, overdrinking, and overwhelming myself with more and more to do.

It wasn't until I created a system of checking in with my purpose consistently and clearing space for what's important to me that I was able to get out of the weeds for good.

If you stick around until the end of this chapter, I'll share what I've learned since then, but first, I'll go a little deeper into what happened next.

When I felt stuck working in my nightmare of a job in news, I began journaling, vision boarding and diving deeper into the art of Manifestation. I spent all my alone time meditating on the idea that a career was waiting for me in Pittsburgh and that I could lead a fulfilling life from there. My only goal was to be home.

So, I moved back in with my parents in April of 2016 and started serving and bartending at The Bulldog Pub where I'd worked during my senior year of college. I found a nannying gig with a wealthy family in a beautiful neighborhood so that I could pull in some extra cash during my off days. They paid me well and I got the perks of hanging out at their fancy Golf Club pool and dining out with them at five-star restaurants. I grew a rainy-day fund, and I was finally making a dent in my growing student loan debt. I could take vacations and afford outings like concerts and festivals. I could devote myself to my friends and family without feeling exhausted and irritable. I was having the time of my life!

Alex and I were social butterflies. We knew how to have fun and weren't afraid to let loose. After a few failed relationships with controlling and overbearing partners, I appreciated that he allowed me to be myself. I'm bubbly and flirtatious by nature, but he never got jealous or lost his temper with me. He always included me and liked showing me off to his friends. I felt like a queen. Life was good, it was exciting, and I was happy.

With this new lease on life, I started making time for things I loved, including taking my camera everywhere and documenting

Chapter 4

everything. I'd applied for a couple of "real" jobs with no luck and admittedly felt a bit discouraged but held on to faith that God was holding out for something better.

That's when an opportunity popped up to produce a documentary for the Clean Pittsburgh Commission. My mom was on the board and told me they were looking for an intern to produce a video for their annual meet and greet. This wasn't a paid gig, but I was making plenty from bartending and babysitting and I was living at home again without a ton of expenses, so I thought to myself, *I've got a camera, I've got a microphone and a tripod, why not me?!*

It sounded fun, so I volunteered. That summer, I must have spent one hundred plus hours shooting more than twenty interviews and collecting footage for this documentary.

I was in my glory piecing this thing together!

Unlike the horror stories of deadly car accidents and devastating fires I'd been forced to share for so long in the news industry, I was able to produce this positively uplifting film that inspired people to clean up our city. During the premiere, the Mayor of Pittsburgh stood up and announced they'd be sharing my video on the City Cable Channel. I was proud and felt as if my future was in my hands. I realized then that I had a service to offer and saw an opportunity to create the life I wanted instead of seeking to find it elsewhere.

Before I knew it, I had my own production company. I made business cards and amped up my website. I developed a pricing guide and got a friend with a law degree to write up a standard contract I could use. I began collecting deposits for upcoming shoots and would put those payments toward purchasing more professional equipment. A friend of mine from college had been producing music videos and wedding films for a few years. His work always inspired me, so I studied it and then volunteered to film the weddings of a few separate couples in the fall of 2016. I announced that I was a wedding videographer, and people believed me.

In the new year, I set a goal to have fourteen weddings under my belt by the end of 2017. Achieving that goal lit a fire inside of me and fueled my belief in the notion that I had the power to do anything and be anyone.

Lucky for me, Alex was an accountant and an expert in all things finance. With his guidance and encouragement, I officially registered my business at the start of 2018 and left my bartending job by the end of September to take it full time. Alex proposed that same month and we got to work planning our wedding. By Christmas 2019, after thirty-one weddings and dozens of other projects that year, plus the to-dos of organizing a wedding of my own, I'd found myself burned out once again. I was in over my head with clients waiting for their unfinished films and photo galleries. I'd achieved everything I'd asked for and more, but I was overwhelmed.

Here's what I've learned since then.

Your Goals Are Not The End

Maybe you've heard the saying, "A goal without a plan is just a wish." I prefer to say,

"A plan without a purpose is a waste of time." I can pinpoint countless instances in my life that I've reached a goal but felt unsatisfied—like all the effort I'd put in was a big waste of energy.

When I reached my goal of becoming a television personality, it didn't bring me the feelings I expected. I mean, maybe it would have if I'd stuck it out for another ten years and made it to *Good Morning America* or ESPN, but would that have been any more fulfilling? The hair and the makeup and the showing up in heels day after day, expected to look and be perfect, just wasn't going to cut it for my life.

I never got to the deeper purpose behind my desire to be on television and pursued surface level goals that made sense. Through that experience and many that followed, I learned a priceless lesson: Our goals are not the end. They provide a *means* to an end. That's why it's important to have a clear purpose behind every goal you set and a loose attachment to any one particular result.

There are infinite roads you can take to achieve the feelings you're hoping to manifest in your life. Because your goals are not the end!

When you're setting goals, start with your purpose, specifically thinking about the feelings that you want to cultivate. How do you want to feel? Why do you want to create whatever it is that you're envisioning for your future? Let that lay the foundation and serve as your mission statement.

Think of your purpose as your North Star and allow your goals to ebb and flow with the seasons of life. You're constantly growing and changing as a human being. It only makes sense that your goals would change too. So, check in with your overarching mission before you take action toward a goal and be sure that goal aligns with your purpose.

Let's say my purpose is to make a global impact by sharing my story through a book that helps people lead happier and healthier lives. Maybe I set a goal to publish a book by the end of the year.

What actions must I take to bring that book to life and how can I make sure that said book aligns with my overarching mission?

Well first things first, I have to write the book, and I don't just want to write a book about anything; I want to write a book that helps people get the most out of life. For all those action takers out there like me, learning to begin at the end with a clear and deeply rooted purpose provides direction when you're on the move toward your goals. If you're going to map out a plan of action, start with your purpose and work backward.

If your purpose isn't clear yet, but you have a specific goal in mind, you can use the seven-layers-deep exercise to get to the heart of your desire. I learned this method back in 2020, when I hired my first business coach, Danielle Langton, and I've been using it ever since.[3]

The Seven-Layers-Deep Exercise

Start with your goal. Maybe you want to leave your nine to five job to start your own creative business as a photographer. Ask yourself,

"Why is it important to leave my job and start my own creative business?"

Maybe you would respond with something like,

"It's important because I want more freedom, joy and flexibility in my daily life and photography makes me happy."

That's great! You're off to a good start already, but let's keep this going to get deeper into the core of your goal.

Ask yourself again,

---

3. You can find a printable version of the Seven Layers Deep Exercise inside of my Journaling Prompts for Joyful Living available at ShannonTheGoodWitch.com/TheHealthyHigh.

Chapter 4

"Why is it important for me to have more freedom, joy and flexibility in my daily life?"

You would probably say something like,

"I want to be available for my friends and family without feeling burned out or overextended. I want to give them the best of me."

That makes total sense! But I know you can go deeper.

So, why is it important to you to be available at your best for your friends and family? Most likely, because you love them, and you want to have the energy to support them and help them to overcome their own obstacles. Now we're getting somewhere!

Why is it important that you have the energy to support your community? If you were asking me, I'd probably say,

"It's because I feel a deep sense of joy and fulfillment when I know my loved ones are healthy and happy."

So, ask again.

"Why is it important to feel joyful and fulfilled?"

"Because I'm my best dang self when I'm happy and my cup is full!"

And one last time for good measure, we'll ask again!

"Why is it important to be your best self?"

And you'd say,

"Because when I'm my best dang self, I'm better able to show up and serve my community and create a ripple effect of positive change in the world!"

So, by really digging deep into your surface level goal of wanting to quit your job and start a business and then peeling the layers of the onion, you discovered that at the end of the day, what you really want is to **have the energy to show up and serve your**

community with your gifts and make a positive impact in the lives of the people who matter most to you.

Being able to clearly state your mission will serve as the driving force behind every action you take. Knowing your purpose and keeping it front of mind will keep you on track when you're faced with difficult decisions. This should feel freeing and expansive!

You'll see that it's not just about leaving your job and starting a business. There are so many different paths you can take to feel like your freest and most expressed self, and now that you know what you're after, you'll be open to any opportunity that arises that aligns with that mission. Focus your attention on your dream of being your highest self and having the time and energy to serve your loved ones. You'll find that the possibilities are endless.

And you might even see that you don't want to start a business because that's going to suck up all the time and energy that you want to be devoting to your loved ones.

Remember: your goals are not the end; they're simply a *means* to an end.

There are infinite paths you can take to get to the same destination. The trick is to keep an open mind. You don't want to get so caught up on one plan that you miss out on all the opportunities Life is throwing your way! Hold tight to your purpose when the going gets tough and seek out silver linings when things don't work out. Everything happening now is leading to the fulfillment of your desires, and it's all meaningful. Try not to sweat the small stuff.

If you're an achiever like me, slow down and reflect often. Absolutely anything is possible for you, so get to the heart of your

Chapter 4

desires. How can you ever expect to feel satisfied if you don't ask for what you're really craving? If you were at a restaurant and you wanted lemonade, you wouldn't ask for lemons, a knife, a cutting board, a juicer, a cup of sugar, and a pot of boiling water to make the simple syrup. As a matter of fact, you'd probably be pretty puzzled if they brought you a big pile of stuff and said,

"Figure it out yourself!"

If you want lemonade, ask for the lemonade!

It's like this in life when you find yourself craving more juice. Rather than demanding what you really want, you ask for all the ingredients you think are going to help you make lemonade. You ask for a new career so that you can make more money so that you can go out and buy all the ingredients to make your sticky-sweet lemonade, but what if you just asked for the lemonade from the very beginning? Maybe someone would have just handed you a glass of freshly squeezed lemonade and saved you a bunch of time figuring out where to get all the ingredients and how to make it yourself. You could spend so much time making money that you forget to go buy the lemonade you wanted in the first place.

Don't overthink it. Get to the bottom of what you really want and ask for that from the get-go!

Yes, you have a divine purpose to fulfill and infinite potential to make a positive impact in this lifetime, but that doesn't mean there's some big thing you have to do or that you're supposed to accomplish before you can kick back and enjoy yourself.

You are innately entitled to a magical life, so let it be easy. [4]

---

[4]. If you're seeking support for your personal growth journey, visit ShannonTheGoodWitch.com/services for a list of my current coaching offers and digital products.

In the next chapter, I'm sharing the story of a time I followed my intuition and stepped into perfect harmony with the Universe. Take a deep breath and flip the page when you're ready to fall into flow.

Maybe you take a moment to reflect before moving on:

Recall a trying time in your past. How has it shaped you? What did you learn? Can you think of an example from your life when you've reached a goal, but at the end of the road, you felt unsatisfied, unfulfilled, and unsure of where to go next? Try the seven-layers-deep exercise to figure out what you were really after when you set that goal. Does the purpose behind it still resonate with you?

CHAPTER 5

Falling into Flow

"When you want something, all the universe conspires to help you achieve it."

—Paulo Coelho, The Alchemist

When I booked my trip to Tamarindo, Costa Rica, in November 2021, I knew I had some healing to do. My friend Jeremy Ehrlich (the same Jeremy I mentioned in Chapter Two) had been living there for six months and I suddenly felt as if I should go and visit him. "Jerm" was the very first friend I made in college when we met during a summer orientation day. He's handsome, with a big, bright smile and soul-piercing eyes. We both studied Broadcast Journalism at Duquesne and connected over our shared interests and spiritual curiosities. I'd never traveled alone, but after all I'd been through that year, I wanted some space to explore my heart and celebrate a fresh start. I had this feeling that Jeremy could help me, so without hesitation, I trusted my intuition and booked my flights a few hours after the idea popped into my head. I didn't worry if the dates would align with Jeremy's plans. I simply trusted that it would all work out.

Costa Rica is an energy vortex, well known for its spiritual healing powers. My intuition must have known this and guided me there. I stepped off the plane to find a beautiful melting pot of people from around the world on spiritual journeys of their own. It felt as if I had suddenly fallen into perfect harmony with the Universe. Each serendipitous moment flowed into the next, perfectly aligned—miracle after miracle unfolding before me—reinforcing my belief that God is, and always has been, working in my favor. All I had to do was surrender.

I spent five days getting to know Jeremy's soulful community, collecting quiet moments to myself between gatherings. Alex came out for the second half of the trip and by the time he arrived, I'd already made a handful of friends, including a middle-aged native named Darwin. I met Darwin on my second day in town when I walked by him on my way to the beach. He was sweeping the patio of a local restaurant and said to me, "Pura vida." He was sweet and funny, and we chatted for ten minutes or so. The interaction was so special that I wrote about it in my journal.

When I ran into him again a few days later, it felt as if the Universe had brought us together for a reason.

This time, he looked different. His tennis shoes were worn, and he carried a backpack. We walked and talked together for a while as he helped me buy some supplies at the convenience store where I was having trouble due to my poor Spanish speaking skills. Somewhere along the way, he told me his temporary job at the restaurant was over and that he would only be given one last night to crash in the dining room, so he was looking for more work. He was getting his resumes printed at a local shop, so I walked with him to pick them up. He was a talented and experienced server, but he didn't have a way for any of these restaurants to get in touch with him, so I offered to buy him a cell phone.

Later, friends warned me that this could be a scam and that he was probably lying to me, but I believed him, and I wanted to help. He came back with me to my beach bungalow tucked into the palm trees, where I would meet up with Jeremy. Darwin showed us magic tricks and kept us laughing and giggling the entire time. We got to know each other and talked about our lives. He told me that he knew he had "power." I could see his potential—He just needed a chance.

To make a very long story a little shorter, I helped Darwin come up with the money to catch a cab to a different town where he had a lead on a potential serving gig. I felt as if I had done something good. My heart was full, and although I'm not sure if Darwin used the money to get to his destination or for something different, it didn't matter. I felt a sense of peace in my heart and knew that I was on the right path—I was exactly where I was meant to be.

It was like a fog had cleared, and I could suddenly see what mattered most. I'd worked all my life to make something of myself so that I could help people, but I'd been so busy working that I hadn't had time to volunteer or raise money for charity in the way I'd always felt called.

That's when it hit me.

I'd spent all my life searching for purpose. There must be some point to it all, right? A reason for being here—some deeper meaning. I'd busied myself with the task of finding this big, mysterious, intangible thing I thought I was supposed to covet and tired myself working to achieve it. I had these grand ideas of who I was supposed to be and what a successful life was supposed to look like. Time and time again, I found myself hung up on mistakes and easily frustrated when things didn't go according to plan. I was harder on myself than I'd ever be on someone else and often felt like a failure for falling short of my own great expectations. I'd been missing out on endless opportunities to experience joy because I was so distracted by that annoying little voice inside of my head that keeps yelling nonsense like, "Shoulda, woulda, coulda!" But, at the end of the day, my purpose is the same as yours:

To love and be loved.

It's really that simple, isn't it?

All that really matters is this moment and what I decide to do with it!

So, if you're like me and you're looking for a purpose in life too, why not choose love?

No matter where you are on your journey, whether you're on the starting line, the finish line, or lost somewhere in the middle, lead with love and you will find your way.

I said goodbye to Darwin and skipped off with Jeremy and Alex to celebrate. We were headed to an "Ecstatic Dance" hosted by a beautiful English girl named Georgia who'd settled in Costa Rica a few years earlier. She handed out cups of hot cacao and we sipped and sat with strangers from all walks of life, awaiting the music to begin. Cacao is the raw, unprocessed form of chocolate, and is said to be a heart opener. Something had certainly opened my heart that night because by the end of the DJs set, I was plugged in and charged up with unbounded energy.

Chapter 5

This was the first time I'd been to a sober dance party, and I was hooked. I'd always loved to dance, but this wasn't just like dancing at a wedding or learning a choreographed number for a performance. The music was groovy and tribal. Sans alcohol, I could move freely without the fear of losing my balance and bumping into people, like I would be if I were drunk. I was ECSTATIC! I felt a deep appreciation for my connection to the Earth, simultaneously liberated and at home in my body.[5]

This was mid-pandemic and a curfew was in place throughout the country, but that didn't stop the locals from throwing late night shindigs or "secret jungle parties." Later that evening, Alex and I hopped in a car with our new acquaintances Edgar, Paula and Rosa, who we'd met at the home of some local musicians who looked and partied like rockstars. We drove off to the jungle, headed to the secret coordinates, and made our way up the mountain where deep and dirty reggae music played from the DJ's speakers. Peering up at the moon—full and bright as the love inside my heart—we danced and drifted between dimensions chanting, "Luna y estrellas!"

An hour before sunrise, Edgar delivered us safely back to our Airbnb where we found Jeremy sitting cross legged on the sofa with a gigantic smile on his face after a profound experience of his own. We were all over the moon that night and I'm still convinced that there's some serious, energetic magic there in Tamarindo, but you don't have to fly off to Guanacaste to connect to it.

This sense of magic resides inside of you and appears when you place your attention on it.

---

5. Ecstatic Dance is a powerful modality for connecting to your intuition and releasing stagnant energy, so if you're feeling curious, head over to ShannonTheGoodWitch.com/Dance for guidance or simply search "ecstatic dance" in your area to find a tribe near you!

The Healthy High

A few days earlier, Jeremy had led me to a morning microdosing ceremony on the beach. We arrived to find a captivating Romanian woman named Ana standing beside colorful pieces of cloth and crystals she'd laid out for us. She was sweet and soft-spoken as she asked our intentions and blessed the mushroom tea she was pouring up for free. I'd always been interested in psilocybin, but had never experimented, so I was excited for the opportunity to try it in the presence of a "Microdosing Guru." We were riding a high from a powerful meditation experience the evening before and celebrating synchronicities left and right.

We were in flow.

I sipped my tea while Ana played music that tugged at my heartstrings. Tears filled my eyes as I journaled on dreams and waded in the water. We closed our circle feeling giggly and grateful, so we stuck around to chat. When I mentioned that I was a photographer, Ana lit up! She'd been looking for me too. I offered to return that evening at sunset to snap some photos of her making a mandala with shells and stones on the beach. I couldn't wait to repay her for her generosity.

Jeremy and I left on cloud nine, carrying the pure magic we'd just experienced into the day ahead. We enjoyed a light lunch, spotted iguanas, and laughed our butts off in the swimming pool. So, when we made it to the beach in perfect timing for golden hour, we celebrated! We splashed in the ocean and danced along the shoreline as I photographed two of the most soulful people that I'd ever met. We ended the evening, sitting in the sand and serenading in the saturated sky, holding hands and howling up at the nearly full Moon.[6]

---

[6]. Find my favorite resources on plant medicine and micro-dosing at ShannonTheGoodWitch.com/TheHealthyHigh.

Chapter 5

That trip to Costa Rica serves as my reminder of what it's like to feel in flow, celebrating life for all its wonder. The people I met in Tamarindo had this loving presence about them as they waved and said, *pura vida*, which means "pure life." My Spanish wasn't good, but it didn't need to be. There's a universal language that we all understand.

In English, it's called *love*.

Sometimes it feels like everything is going right, as if you're in effortless harmony with the world around you. You're receiving all the support you could ever need. In Sanskrit, this is called *Kriya* and it's an indication that you're in alignment with your dharma.

Picture this:

You're full of energy. You're bursting with ideas! You're so inspired that you can't wait to jump out of bed in the morning to get going. It's as if you're seeing the world through a pair of rose-colored glasses. The food tastes better, the grass looks greener, you feel deeply connected to the world around you. Your relationships are flourishing. Your health is at its peak. You're overjoyed by a sense of purpose and enthusiasm for your work! Your days are full of meaningful coincidences, it seems as if everything is effortlessly falling into place, and you're in awe of the magic you're experiencing. A deep sense of harmony resonates within you. Your heart feels full, and you just can't help but smile.

This is what flow feels like. Those meaningful coincidence and feelings of alignment are signs from the Universe that you're on the right track.

Think back to a time that you felt deeply satisfied and in sync with the world around you. Where were you? What were you up to? Who were you with? Grab your journal and take a minute to jot down some fond memories of a period that you felt in flow.

I've learned that things rarely turn out exactly how I planned them in my head, but that's the fun in it! There's magic to be discovered around every corner. You simply have to be present.

Before we move into Chapter Six: Opening up, I want to remind you that God is on your side, even when things feel difficult. Opposite of those blissful moments of flow—when everything magically seems to work out and it's easy to feel loved and supported by the Universe—sometimes we experience more challenging seasons and feel like we just can't catch a break.

Through the trials and tribulations, it's important to remember that God isn't punishing you. You're simply being redirected! Trust that everything happening now is leading to your highest good.

In the following chapter, I'm sharing my experience through a tough time that induced the long overdue birth of this book.

CHAPTER 6

Opening Up

It was 5:00 a.m. on a Tuesday in August 2023. Alex and I had just finished packing up the car for a road trip to Pensacola, Florida when our seventeen-year-old rescue cat Sonnie started walking in circles. Everything we read on Google said it could be a neurological problem and told us to take him straight to the vet, so we drove to Med Vet where we'd taken our cat Julie two years earlier. After a few hours in the waiting room, they got him all checked in and recommended that he stay the night for testing. We signed some papers and paid the $2,500 bill with faith that they'd take good care of our little old man who'd already lost his vision a few months earlier. It turns out his blood pressure had skyrocketed to 290 when it should have been 130, so they gave him some medicine and kept him for more testing.

About a week earlier, we found out that Alex's mom had been diagnosed with low-grade Lymphoma and his dad was having surgery to have his prostate removed. They've both since made a full recovery, but at the time, Alex was extra shaken up. Luckily, our second property wouldn't have guests checking in until the weekend, so we settled there for a night while we patiently waited for Sonnie's appointment the next day.

When we returned to the vet, Sonnie seemed frail and exhausted. The sweet vet tech gave us instructions for administering his new blood pressure meds and we got to take him home. There was no way in heck we were going to pack him into the car and drive him to Pensacola in this condition, so we canceled our trip and booked a hotel in Downtown Pittsburgh for the weekend.

Leading up to this point, we'd spent the spring and summer months bouncing between our two short-term rental properties. If they were both booked, we'd pack up our stuff, deep clean the houses and take a spontaneous weekend trip or stay with friends or family. Our semi-nomadic lifestyle had been going well, but this emergency had us questioning how we'd keep it up moving forward. We'd spent ten weeks traveling the country at the start of the year and were considering buying a house in the woods or at the beach that we'd turn into a vacation rental. We'd found success with our Pittsburgh properties and knew we could have another successful Airbnb, but nothing had fallen into place and interest rates were through the roof, so we just kept bouncing around and making do.

After an expensive weekend stay in the teeniest, tiniest, pet friendly hotel room where poor Sonnie had explosive diarrhea from the new medicine, we realized that we'd have to make a decision pretty quickly. Both of our homes had tons of upcoming bookings and we really didn't want to cancel on our guests. The income from Airbnb was easily covering both of our mortgages and all the utilities, plus we were earning a profit every single month. We had no interest in taking them off the market, but we were craving stability. I started researching apartments and a week later, we had the keys to our new studio in the heart of the city. We were sure that our friends and family would think we were crazy, but it made sense to us and we acted on our intuition.

The building sat on the edge of the river with breathtaking views and nature trails. It had a gym and a yoga studio on the first floor and a beautiful community "Club Room" overlooking the city skyline. It was just two buildings over from my mom's apartment building and we loved staying with her and using all the amenities from time to time over the summer. Plus, we saw the potential in settling into Pittsburgh's Strip District neighborhood and utilizing the area as a creative workspace for our businesses.

Alex had left his accounting job about eighteen months earlier and ventured out on his own, so now that we were both entrepreneurs, we were excited to have a place to focus on our work and host our clients. This was a perfect meeting space and a well-lit spot for photoshoots, so we knew we could make the most of our spontaneous decision to rent an apartment for a year while we figured out our next move.

We were sad about canceling our trip to Florida and stressed about the unexpected expenses, but we found a silver lining. We weren't meant to be at the beach—we were supposed to find this space that would propel us in the direction of our dreams.

Through this experience, we gained a new perspective. We hadn't even realized how distracted we'd been all year by catering to our renters and living out of suitcases on other people's time. It was fun while it lasted, but we were limiting ourselves.

Suddenly, life felt expansive and full of possibility. Having somewhere to ground down and settle in freed up our energy and headspace for what was coming next.

Since then, we've recognized all the ways we can live nomadically and travel the world, even with an old blind cat that needs meds twice a day. We don't need to buy another property, we can rent with low stakes and move on when we're ready for a change.

Now, when we're navigating big life decisions, we remember that we don't want more stuff. We want more freedom and free time to devote to what matters most. So, when things don't go to plan (and they very rarely do) maybe God is trying to show you that there's something better coming along—Something you wouldn't have seen had you continued down the weeded path you were walking.

Can you recall a time in your past when absolutely nothing went according to plan, but you rolled with the punches, adapted, and things ended up working out for the better? What happened? What did you learn?

This extra space that we'd created freed up some of the physical and mental energy I'd been exerting all year, scrubbing surfaces and jumping between properties. The fog lifted and fresh ideas popped into my brain. Two weeks after we moved in, I borrowed the book *You Are a Badass at Making Money* from my friend Maddie's shelf while I was checking on her pets. Another six weeks or so had passed before I finally sat down to read it. I loved Jen Sincero's writing, so I blew through the book in a few days' time and appreciated the reminder of my insanely powerful mind and ability to manifest money rather than hustling for it.

Chapter 6

I set a goal on November 8th, 2023 to manifest $50,000 by February 8th, 2024. Three months felt believable and gave me something specific to work toward, so I added a reminder into my Google Calendar and pasted "$50,000" onto my laptop background along with some photos of the life I was calling in. Within the week, I remembered that Alex had applied for a line of credit on our house a year earlier for $42,000. We hadn't pulled on it yet, so we pressed a button and the money appeared in my account. In just fourteen days, I'd already manifested a giant chunk of my goal. Yes, it was a loan and I'd have to make a monthly payment with a bit of interest, but this experience unlocked even more trust in my divine power and gave me the permission I'd been waiting for to go all in.

I hired Laurnie Wilson, a hypnotherapist that I'd been wanting to work with for an entire year and suddenly had this extra layer of support that I'd been craving. My second session with Laurnie landed just after Christmas on the day I'd host my final Full Moon gathering of the year, where I guided my community through an end of year journaling workshop. This workshop gave me a chance to do some reflecting on my own and showed me that I was finally ready to commit to publishing my book. So on January 7th, I signed up for a "30 Day Book Writing Challenge" and set another goal to finish the first draft by February 8th. I knew that I wouldn't be publishing it for a while and didn't expect to make any money on it yet but had a good feeling that this would help me attract that final $8,000 that hadn't arrived in my bank account yet. About a week later, my dad sent me a check for $3,000 and just like that, I was only five thousand away from my goal.

As the month of February approached and I packed my bags for San Francisco to meet my new Godson, Vorn, and celebrate my best friend, Maeve's birthday, I felt good about the money I'd already manifested. I figured that I'd probably earned close to the outstanding $5,000 in other forms of income through my multiple businesses and wiped my hands clean of the pressure to call in that final bit in some magical way. I was dang close to reaching my goal and nearly finished with my first draft, so I called it a double win and flew off to California with my mom to celebrate.

During our few days away, I mentioned to my mom that I was worried about my dad. I hadn't heard back from him after he missed my Aunt Camile's birthday party in January and although it was common for us to go long spurts without chatting on the phone or getting together, I had a feeling something might be wrong. On February 5th, as we were boarding our flight back to Pittsburgh, I was relieved to get a text from my dad about an old Canon camera he'd seen at the thrift shop. He asked if I wanted it and how much I thought it was worth. I politely declined, thanked him for thinking of me and told him I wasn't sure, but I was looking forward to our next get together. I could tell by the following few texts that he was off the wagon. We got home from the airport late that night and instead of following up with my dad, I got back to writing. My manuscript just needed a few finishing touches, so I was excited to wrap up after a long weekend away. Over the next nine days, my soul poured into my writing and by the early morning hours of February 15th, I'd finished my book—or so I thought.

That very same morning, just after 8:00 a.m., my mom called to tell me my dad passed away. My cousin Tim had gone looking for

Chapter 6

my dad at his apartment after a few days of trying to reach him on the phone, with no luck. When there was no answer at the door, Tim called the police who found him seated on the coach. The coroner concluded that he'd likely passed away on the 5th or 6th. My heart hurt, but I felt grateful that we'd texted on his final day and took comfort in the relief that he was finally at peace.

When Alex and I went to his apartment to gather up his belongings, we found $2,000 cash and a bank statement showing $3,000 in his account that would become my inheritance.

A total of $5,000.

This wasn't a coincidence. It was God's way of telling me I was on the right path, so I used this sense of heartbreak to channel even more purpose into my story. My dad would be proud to know that the last of his money went to fulling my passion and passing on his legacy.

My dad's death confirmed what I'd always known to be true: **We all serve a powerful purpose.** He wasn't some upstanding citizen that went out volunteering or walking in peace marches, but by being himself and in being my dad, he made an impact.

In the final few years of his life, my dad had become the loving and generous father that I know he always wanted to be. He sent me cards and checks in the mail and brought Alex and me treasures from the local thrift shop every time we got together for a family gathering or an Eat'n Park outing. After treating us to lunch, he'd take us to the grocery store and pay for our carts. He and my mom made their peace in those final years too, so he'd invite her along and she'd come for the free groceries. Every few months, we'd meet at my grandparents' for dinner and he'd bring a giant pot of his homemade chili. My Pappy and Granny appreciated his deliveries and help around the house. His entire family loved him unconditionally, despite the alcoholism and he loved them, despite the mean and abrasive words he'd say after too many drinks.

Our relationship was complicated, but I wouldn't be the person I am today if my dad weren't himself. I'm grateful that in the end, we got to be friends.

In her book *Discover Your Dharma*, Sahara Rose says, "Your job is not to sacrifice this lifetime to be of service, but to make your highest expression your form of service. When you change your world, you change the world."

The small shifts you make in your daily life will compound overtime. Every decision you make causes a domino effect. Living your purpose isn't about this one grandiose thing you're supposed to do in your lifetime—Your purpose lies in your daily actions. So, explore your desires, learn from your experiences, and express yourself with integrity.

To conclude this chapter, I'd love to share some life lessons I learned from my cat, Sonnie.

Four Keys to a Good, Long Life:

1. Prioritize daily fresh air and movement
2. Drink lots of water
3. Communicate
4. Be friendly

When our kitty Julie passed away in 2021, she made room for the newest addition to our family. Our next-door neighbors were moving and didn't want to take their outdoor cat (Sonnie) away from his stomping grounds. Sonnie paid us regular visits, and even made himself cozy in our bed a few times over the years while making his morning rounds for treats and scratches, up and down the block. We loved his company, so that winter, he moved in with us!

Sonnie is the most vocal cat I know and drinks more water than most cats. He'll tell you exactly what he wants and won't shut up until he gets it, especially when he wants the water dripping out of the faucet so he can snag a slurp. Now that he's blind, he can't go out for his daily walks without his leash and a guardian, but he doesn't let that stop him from meowing at the door and demanding that we open it, so he can sniff the fresh air. He's the most puuurrrfect, loving boy, and is friendly with all the neighbors. People know, love, and trust Sonnie, so they take care of him.

This is a perfect example of the relationship between dharma and manifestation.

Sonnie lives his dharma! His way of expressing himself and being so stinkin' cute and funny, raises the vibrations of everyone he meets. He's a cat, so he's obviously not thinking about all the grand ways he's supposed to help people, but by being himself and demanding what he wants, he gets it, and he lifts people's spirits along the way!

By being yourself, going after what you want, and raising your own vibrations, you're doing your divine part to bring the collective into balance. When you live your dharma, the Universe rewards you, because it wants you to keep going!

So, living your dharma, must then, be the key to unlocking your divine manifestation powers.

If you want all your dreams to come true, be kind, be open, and be YOU!

In Chapter Seven: Own Your Magic, you'll gain a deeper understanding of your one-of-a-kind superpowers and all the divine opportunities that come when you share them with the world.

CHAPTER 7

Own Your Magic

"What you seek is seeking you!"

— Rumi

No matter how much I believe in the power of manifestation and my ability to co-create with the Universe, witnessing my visions come to life never fails to amaze me. When I started a Pittsburgh branch of Happy Hippie Foundation, I wanted a place to bring people together with a desire to bridge gaps and build connections in my hometown. Happy Hippie Foundation is a non-profit organization founded by Miley Cyrus with a mission to rally young people to fight injustice facing homeless youth, LGBTQ+ youth, and other vulnerable populations. If you know me, you'd have reason to believe that I started a branch of Happy Hippie because of my longtime crush on Miley or because I identify as bi-sexual and albeit, you wouldn't be wrong, my why runs so much deeper than that. Growing up with gay family members and queer friends showed me that life wasn't always easy for my LGBTQ+ brothers and sisters or other minority populations. I know that coming out is terrifying and that being "different" can feel isolating and lonely. Pride is spreading across the globe, but even in the United States where we preach freedom and equality, there's still prejudice that stems from fear and a lack of understanding.[7]

When I hosted my first few Happy Hippie events, I didn't know what to expect and I wasn't sure anyone would show up. The response stunned me, and I suddenly knew for certain that there's a gigantic group of people I don't even know yet who are seeking the same thing as me—community, friendship, and a sober space to express themselves!

If there's a dream in your heart, even if it feels far-fetched or impossible, know that it's calling you for a reason. There are people out there looking for YOU and what you have to offer! People need to know who you are. They need to hear your story. You're not going to be for everyone, but the more fully you express yourself and the more confidently you share your message, the easier it's going to be to attract people who support you!

Take a moment to reflect on your passions.

What excites you? What lights you up? What turns you on? What inspires you? What fills you with so much energy that you just can't contain it? What could you spend hours doing just for fun? What do you do that leaves you feeling fulfilled?

A month before my first Happy Hippie "Golden Hour Get Together" to celebrate the Summer Solstice in 2023, I'd picked

---

7. Please join our community on Instagram @happyhippiefdnPGH and reach out to get involved or register for email updates about Happy Hippie Community Events at ShannonTheGoodWitch.com/gettogethers.

Chapter 7

up a laid-back gig at my friend Maddie Rigatti's Jewelry Shop to supplement my income while I developed my coaching practice. The shop sat inside of a building full of commercial spaces with floor to ceiling windows for local artists and small business owners. The donut shop brought in tons of foot traffic, so the place was bustling with friendly hipsters from the up-and-coming neighborhood.

While I held down the fort a few days a month, I got to meet new people and absorb the vibrant energy of this hub for community and creativity. There, I attracted soulful people who wanted to support me too! Some of them attended my Happy Hippie events, others booked me for branding sessions, and several joined The Good Coven, my container for spiritual women.[8]

I suddenly had this network of kind and loving humans who showed up for me when I needed them. When my dad passed away, these new friends brought me flowers and attended the funeral. I was suddenly surrounded by magical individuals with loving hearts and a desire to serve because I called them in through self-expression. I could hardly believe that, in less than one calendar year, I'd cultivated this life full of so much loving support from my peers.

I owe my ability to attract the kind of people who love me for me, to my personal brand. When I was transitioning out of weddings and into my new role as a Spiritual Life Coach, I knew that claiming the name Shannon~The Good Witch and sharing my love for magic would attract magical people, so I hired a Brand Designer to help me bring my vision to life. Thanks to Ayesha Santo's professional guidance and authentic approach to brand and website design, I

---

8. If you're interested in learning more about The Good Coven or other ways that we can work together, visit ShannonTheGoodWitch.com/services.

stepped into my new role as a coach with clarity in my message, confidence in my gifts, and a direct means to spread love and attract my soul tribe!

My given name is Shannon Marie Chavez and I love it so much that I didn't even consider changing it when I got married, but my last name is tough for people to pronounce. Chavez means "key maker" so I like to think that I'm honoring the legacy of my ancestors, who were likely key makers, by opening doors for my community and people around the world that I'll touch with this book. I can't remember when I came up with the name Shannon~The Good Witch, but I knew that it was catchy and something people would remember, so I changed my Instagram handle and printed little moon ritual cards to pass out with my QR code.

And it worked!

My friend Maddie, who owns the jewelry shop I worked in for a time, is a passionate connector and loved tagging me in her posts for her shop. Every time I was working, or she shared a photo that I'd taken at one of her markets, she'd give me a shoutout. Soon, all the other vendors in her circle knew me as Shannon~The Good Witch and I was calling in new creative clients left and right. After taking some photos of a real-life witch named Sabrina and her cat named Salem, I got an email telling me that someone had signed up for The Good Coven. Sabrina was my first witch and all we needed to call in the rest of our Coven. Within a few months, we had attracted nine more witches and now, I have a flourishing community of magical beings of all kinds pouring into my realm.

Chapter 7

When I'm meeting with my Brand Photography clients ahead of a Portrait Session, I use the acronym **M.A.G.I.C** to help them gain clarity on their "superpowers." Together, we break down the word M.A.G.I.C as we work to pinpoint their unique dharma—the way in which they're meant to show up and serve. As a photographer and coach, it's my mission to help my clients build their "know, like, and trust factor." I want the images that we capture and the message we crystalize to highlight their value and speak to the people who need them.[9]

You don't have to have a business to create a personal brand for yourself. I'd love for you to use this technique on your own to get to know yourself on a deeper level.

Own your M.A.G.I.C.

M is for Mission and Message
A is for Adversity and Aesthetic
G is for Gifts and Guilty Pleasures
I is for Influence and Inspiration
C is for Connection and Credibility

Mission and Message: What is the purpose behind everything you do and what do you hope to express through your work? What message do you want to get across? Why is this your mission? Why do you want to share this message?

Adversity and Aesthetic: What obstacles have you overcome to get to where you are now? What challenges are you still facing or helping

---

[9]. Be sure to follow along with my photography account on Instagram @TheGoodWitchCreative.

others to move through? Next, think about your visual aesthetic. What's your brand style? Neutral or colorful? Sleek and modern or eclectic and bohemian? Let people see you for who you are.

Gifts and Guilty Pleasures: What are you naturally good at? How do you help people without even trying? What do you love to do that maybe you're a little embarrassed about? All these things make you YOU and can help you add value to other people's lives if you let them. Highlight your genius and get comfortable sharing even the taboo topics if it means that you can reach the people who need your help!

Influence and Inspiration: Whether you realize it or not, you are influencing the people around you. You are making an impact on the world with every action you take! Get really clear on who you're influencing and what you're putting out there so that you can make an intentional impact. Consider where you get your inspiration now. Look to your teachers, role models and favorite places for ideas when it comes to designing your own personal brand!

Connection and Credibility: What is it that makes you relatable? What key components of your life or personality are going to strike a chord with people? Make connections and own your accolades. We want people to trust you and they certainly will if you're consistently providing knowledge and value. Don't be afraid to toot your own horn! Let people know why they should choose you over another product or service provider. They're going to stick around if you continue to show up authentically and serve.

Chapter 7

Take a moment here to tap into your superpowers. What are you innately good at without training or explanation? What unique circumstances have you experienced? What are your natural born gifts? What can you do in your sleep? When people compliment you, what do they say? When they come to you for help or advice, what are they asking you about?

Living my purpose fills me up and sustains me. It's the greatest high of all! When I'm living in alignment with my dharma, I feel energized and able to give. So, follow your bliss and lean into the moments that you're feeling fulfilled.

Maybe somewhere along the way you learned to suppress parts of yourself in order to accommodate another person's needs or expectations, but when you act out of fear or obligation, you'll feel drained, empty, bored and uninspired.

When you act of our pure love and authenticity, your energy is inexhaustible!

Who are you when no one is watching, when your guard is down and you have full permission to be 100% you? List out a few uncomfortable truths about yourself. And these can be things that you might feel embarrassed to share with others out of fear of being judged, or maybe you wouldn't want your parents or an authority figure like your boss to know. What parts of yourself are you afraid to let others see? Have you been hiding or suppressing any thoughts or emotions? Are you keeping any secrets? Open up in your journal.

You are innately valuable. Your one-of-a-kind energy is worth more than you think!

Be yourself, claim your worth, and you will prosper.

In Chapter Fifteen: Manifesting Money, I'll share the exact method I use for inviting more wealth into my life (because let's be real, in this modern-day world, money might be the closest thing we have to magic) but first, I'd like to give a shoutout to my accountant. . .

After building up a record of getting fired from his traditional jobs—jobs that he never really loved in the first place—Alex, my husband, took a new role as "The Controller" of an engineering company. This new job was an upgrade from his last and came with his own office, lining him up to become Chief Financial Officer when the current, eighty-something-year-old CFO was ready to retire. He accepted the gig and started with enthusiasm, but after a few months, quickly realized that he was falling into the same pattern of feeling frustrated with his higher ups for failing to take him seriously.

Alex is a *master* with all things money and has a knack for finding creative ways to save it or grow it (and that's not just a figure of speech). One of his old jobs paid for his online graduate program at a branch campus of Louisiana State University. By the time he graduated with his Master of Business Administration, he had no debt, and actually made money through some kind of education credit he applied to his tax return. He studied during Covid while starting up some side hustles, like selling his old Pokémon cards and collectable items on eBay. Soon enough, he had a whole new side business on top of all the accounting help he'd been providing to me and his friends.

Chapter 7

So, while I was studying for my coaching certificates, I decided to use him for practice! I asked him all kinds of questions about his vision for the future. After a hectic year of wedding planning and prioritizing other people, we'd re-emerged in 2022 with a focus on our relationship. We brainstormed our bucket list items and decided that we wanted more freedom to travel the world. He was already worth a third of a million dollars, so why was he holding onto this job and fancy title that wouldn't grant him the flexibility to work online?

A month or so into my program, I was introduced to a modality called Human Design that's based on "The Science of Differentiation." We were using it to gain insight into our unique energetic blueprint to reflect and help our clients embody their dharma. Based on my time and location of birth, I'm a 6/2 Projector. I won't expand on the details of my reading, but I will tell you that my chart resonated with me so deeply that I spiraled down a rabbit hole that week, compiling research for all my closest loved ones, based on their charts.

Human Design highlights something called "channels" that run between our "energy centers" and can be used to give us insight into our innate gifts. Alex was a 6/2 Manifestor and only had one channel showing up in his chart. It was "The Channel of Money." When I walked him through this astoundingly accurate reading, he could finally see the potential in himself to leave his demanding job and go all in on his businesses! Later that Summer, he gave his notice and transitioned out of his role and into his own.[10]

---

[10]. My favorite Human Design related resources are available at ShannonTheGoodWitch.com/TheHealthyHigh where you can also find Alex's contact info. You can follow him directly at @AlTheAlchemist_ on Instagram and Tik-Tok or at AGO Financial LLC on Facebook.

Just like that, I had my first official coaching success story!

Watching Alex blossom into this new entrepreneurial version of himself and seeing him so full of pride for his work, transformed our relationship. I can't help but listen in when I hear him on the phone with his clients. It's so clear that he's living his purpose. He's the same cool, charming, guy that he is around his friends and has a knack for making them feel safe, supported and certain about their financial future. He completely lights up when he's helping people!

Life is slow-paced these days. Alex and I spend our mornings making breakfast and sipping coffee on the couch while brainstorming new business ideas and talking about our dreams. We schedule intentional time together, taking walks, doing yoga, making art, and snuggling with our cat in front of the TV. We're deeply in love and truly can't get enough of each other. After nine years, it seems that we've molded into one, whole being while simultaneously growing more and more into our own uniqueness.

Like me, Al wears a lot of hats, but there are very few we share. We both pull our weight around the house, but besides cooking meals together and taking turns on the dishes, we each have our own set of chores and household responsibilities.

Alex adheres to the exact same routine every single week, practically to the tee. On Sundays, he does the grocery shopping and picks up only the supplies we need for the week or foreseeable future. He plans our meals and makes sure we have enough to make a week's worth for two. We don't really like going out to eat since we've got such a good system at home. Alex likes to cook, but he really loves to save money, so if we can prepare healthy meals at home for two bucks a plate, it feels crazy going out to eat and spending thirty dollars on food that often leaves us feeling sluggish and bloated.[11]

Now that we're both entrepreneurs and we get to wake up and do exactly what we choose, we've built an effortless routine that suits us and gives us freedom to create!

Maybe I'll share the details of how I manifested Alex in a future book, but for now, if you resonate with this story, take it as your sign to follow your callings and lean into your God-given gifts. You don't have to leap! The small steps you take in the direction of your dreams will get you far in time.

I remember imagining a life like this—it's still surreal watching it unfold. Now, it's my mission to help you make your dreams come true too!

Think of me like Glinda, The Good Witch, from *The Wizard of Oz*. I don't grant wishes; I give you the power to grant them yourself, by showing you that "you've always had the power." It's always been inside of you, and it will always be there. You have everything you need to transform your life!

It just takes practice and a little practical magic.

In Part Two: Harnessing Your Innate Power, I'm mapping out the very rituals that I've used to heal and grow. You won't have to keep swimming against the current if you learn to ride the waves.

The water is warm. Dive in when you're ready!

---

11. You can snag our grocery list at ShannonTheGoodWitch.com/TheHealthyHigh.

PART TWO: Harnessing Your Innate Power

CHAPTER 8
Thoughts Become Flesh

Whether you believe it or not, your thoughts are creating your reality. There's a give and take when it comes to everything you do. A push and pull. A cause and effect. You get to play a role in the process.

Things don't just happen to you. You're making them happen with your subconscious mind—a lifetime of stories you've learned through society that make up who you are and what you think and believe to be true.

But you are not your thoughts.

When you realize that your thoughts are separate from you and you start to pay attention to what's on your mind, you can begin to take control of what you're thinking about and shift the effect you have on the world around you.

Your thoughts emit a frequency, like a radio, and you're tuning into other frequencies that are playing on the same channel. Like attracts like, after all. So what you're thinking about, you're bringing about. It's called The Law of Attraction. Simple right? If you don't like what you're hearing on the other end, change the channel. It's just like this with life—if you don't like what you're getting, change the signal you're putting out.

Let me break it down to you this way:

Your thoughts create your emotions.

Your emotions trigger your actions.

Your actions determine your results.

When we map it out like this, it's easy to see that our thoughts create our realities. I'll share an example from my formative years with an encouraging, yet overbearing mother whose mission in life was to help me succeed.

I went to a performing arts school from sixth through twelfth grade. Our mascot was a unicorn and our colors were rainbow. I knew I was fortunate to be at a school like this where kids expressed themselves without fear of judgment. We were taught to be weird and different.

Lots of the kids at my school were immensely talented at their craft. I wasn't bad at any of the things I tried, but I never had one stand out talent or passion. My attention was always split.

I liked softball and I was pretty good at it, but when I moved out of the slow-pitch league and into fast-pitch, I got a new coach and he was kind of a jerk, so I quit the team and gave my all to cheerleading. My mom despised cheerleading, however, and always discouraged me from pursuing it in a competitive format. She didn't like the catty girls and cheer moms and wanted me to pursue something more worthwhile, so she sent me to summer camps with wealthy, suburban kids where I learned to play the harp and perform in musicals. I felt privileged to have all these opportunities, but the older I got, the less clarity I had.

Chapter 8

Heading into high school, I knew that music wasn't my thing and decided to switch my major from piano to dance, with help from my mom who choreographed my audition number. I loved dancing and was accepted into the program without any formal training. By the end of the year, my mom decided that dance wasn't going to get me anywhere in life and pushed me to change my major again to theater. After one year of falling in love with dance and quickly leveling up to the girls who'd been dancing their entire lives, I had to audition, yet again, for a different major. I was sad to leave my friends and teachers in dance, but part of me believed that my mom was right—I probably wouldn't go on to be a professional dancer—so I made the best of the situation and practiced for another audition.

My mom got a kick out of being involved in this kind of stuff, so she picked my song and monologue and coached me through the process. Once again, she'd successfully helped me get into the program where I'd stay for the next three years, getting a well-rounded education in theater and making the most amazing friends. I settled for one dance class a week among a variety of improv and Shakespeare classes that terrified me. I wasn't as good at theater as I was at dance, so my confidence plummeted, but I stepped up to the plate and did my best to grow despite that every time I performed, my heart pounded out of my chest and caused me to visibly shake. But I pushed through the fear and became a teacher's pet in most of my classes.

My mom always told me that I should strive to be "the best." Not "the best that I could be," but that I should always aim to be "the best" at everything I tried. But how could I be the best at so many things? I was still trying to figure out what I liked and what

I was good at and the couple of things that I felt like I could be the best at—dance and cheerleading—weren't suitable options in her opinion. It was a constant battle. She had a bad temper and could very easily turn from the sweetest, most pleasant mom in the world to a screaming Medusa with twelve heads. I wanted to keep the peace, so I tried to behave and make her happy.

Don't get me wrong, I appreciated that my mom cared and I did love my theater classes. I enjoyed getting to try so many avenues of the performing arts, but I certainly never felt like the best at anything and adopted the belief that if I wanted to get to the top, that I'd have to work hard. I could see that practice paid off and that even though music and theater didn't come as naturally to me as dancing, repetition and dedication led to progress. If I put in the effort and worked at something long enough, I could succeed and gain the approval of my mom and my teachers.

Other things I loved doing in my free time included arts and crafts, like drawing and making handmade greeting cards. I loved styling my friends' hair, drawing tattoos on their bodies and doing their makeup, but although my mom's best friend had become a successful hair stylist with his own salon, my mom wouldn't even allow me to consider going to cosmetology school.

Besides, I didn't really know that entrepreneurship was a possibility. I was going to college, whether I wanted to or not, so I didn't fight it or question it. I was a smart kid with a good head on my shoulders and I knew that college would propel me forward and get me out of the house.

I loved the idea of being out on my own. I didn't want to have to answer to my mom the rest of my life. I was ready to make my own decisions and prove that I could be independently successful.

Chapter 8

Somewhere along the line, my mom came up with the idea that I should go into meteorology. Since I excelled in my science classes and I probably wasn't going to become a famous actress, she thought it would be a good use of my performance skills in a field that she could understand. She's a huge news watcher and wanted to see me on TV someday. Meteorology was a little too specialized and only available at a few Universities in Pennsylvania. I'd have to stay in state to receive a $20,000 Pittsburgh Promise scholarship for graduating from the Pittsburgh Public School system.[12] The options were limited, so we settled on Duquesne University, a Tier 1 school with a great Broadcast Journalism program, just a few miles from home. I took out loans for campus housing without any idea what compound interest meant, and joyfully moved in, ready to begin my adult life at the young age of seventeen-years-old.

I'm a social being and good at making friends, so I instantly became a part of a community. I got a job as a campus tour guide and had the best time walking around with visiting high school students and their parents, showing them what we had to offer. I volunteered to be a team leader for freshman orientation and took advantage of every opportunity to be involved because my mom always said, "It's all about who you know." I networked my way into rooms with people who inspired me and attracted a diverse group of purpose-driven students to help me in my creative endeavors. With the help of gifted peers, a willing team of faculty, and unlimited resources funded by doners and tuition, I had everything I needed to launch a Youtube show called "Dukes All Access" where I interviewed **coaches and athletes, shot gameday highlights, and filmed post-game** interviews for the entire athletic department.

---

12. The Pittsburgh Promise is so much more than a scholarship! Learn more about their mission at PittsburghPromise.org.

I worked just as hard as I played and strived to be the best at everything I did, just as my mom taught me. I was finally doing things on my own terms and took pride in my collegiate success. But all this socializing and studying made it difficult to hear my heart. Roommates, sorority sisters, frat parties, and projects captivated my attention and my journal, where I did the most self-discovery, fell to the side.

By the end of my four years in college, I thought that I wanted to be a famous sportscaster and built up the skills and resume to do it. I believed that I could get there if I continued to give it my all, so I accepted that crappy news job so that I could work my way up the ladder toward a dream that wasn't my own.

Can you see how it was my learned beliefs that created my results? It wasn't until I made space in my days to reconnect to the voice of my highest self that I realized I'd gotten so far off track from my deep desire to help people.

Take a moment to pause and reflect:

What's going on around you? How do you feel about your current circumstances? What has happened recently as a result of the actions that you've taken over the past few years? Can you see the relationship between your thoughts, feelings, and actions?

If you feel like you're ready to shed some limiting beliefs and pave a new path forward, that's amazing—I'm here for it! With practice, you can harness the power of your thoughts to create the life you want, but be aware, you're not going to be able to change a lifetime of subconscious programming overnight.

Chapter 8

It takes commitment and repetition.

If you practice something enough, it becomes automatic. Like when I learned to play "The Entertainer" on the piano as a kid for a school audition. I could play that song forward and backward, completely from memory after a few months of dedicated practice. The judge over my audition, Mrs. Keeney, who would go on to be my piano teacher for the next three years through middle school, caught on. She could tell I was playing from memory, so she pointed to the sheet music in front of me and had me play from the notes. I fumbled through the piece. So, if I couldn't read the music, how was I able to play the song without a flaw on my first attempt?

Because my subconscious mind absorbed it. The song became ingrained in my muscles. My fingers knew exactly what to do. I didn't have to think about it anymore because I had practiced it so many times!

Thoughts become flesh.

Lucky for you, my manifestation ritual is so easy that before long, you won't even have to think about it! Once you get the hang of it, your brain will change on a subconscious level. Thinking constructive thoughts that align with your dreams will become second nature and soon, you'll start to notice all the divine opportunities you've been attracting all along.

With that, remember you're human and you're meant to experience a full range of human emotions. You don't have to be positive all the time to attract the life you want, but when you have mantras and rituals that ground you and bring you home to the truth of who you are and what you have the power to do in this lifetime, it's going to be a heck of a lot easier to shift back into that flow state when those pesky negative thoughts creep in.

The Healthy High

Keep reading if you're ready to create some new healthy thinking habits.

CHAPTER 9
You Are a Divine Creator

Your mind never shuts up. If that voice in your head were your roommate, you'd think they were crazy and annoying, and you'd probably tune them out. But we entertain our thoughts for days, months, and years on end! Why? Because we think we're listening to ourselves. But you are so much more than your mind. You are consciousness.[13]

You have always been here, you will always be here, and when your soul leaves your body, you will take a new form.

The manifestation ritual you're about to learn is all about tuning into the ever-present energy that makes up everything and receiving divine guidance from Source.

I know manifestation feels magical, but really, it's about taking *aligned, decisive action* toward your goals. There's a misconception that manifestation is just about sitting around and thinking about what you want, and that it will simply come to you because you visualized

---

13. In his book, The Untethered Soul, Michael A. Singer expands on this metaphor and explores the concept of consciousness.

it; although seeing it in your mind is a giant piece of the puzzle, you're going to have to *act*!

The key to manifestation though, is taking inspired action that aligns with your innate gifts.

Think of a spider. When a spider is hungry, it casts a web. It doesn't go out hunting. It does what feels natural and creates a web to catch its food. So, when you're figuratively "hungry" for something in life and you're feeling called to do something about it, do what feels natural. When you're manifesting, it's important to trust your intuition, just like a spider casting a web, and to do what comes easily to you rather than looking outside of yourself for direction. You may not be able to cast a beautiful, intricate web like a spider, but I guarantee there's something you could create that would attract what you're craving.

What is your intuition guiding you to do? What action are you feeling called to take?

And maybe you're not like me and you hate spiders and when you see one in your house, you kill it and destroy its web. When I see a spider web in my apartment, I leave it there and let the spider be. On the other hand, if I'm cleaning one of my rental properties, I'll pick up the spider and gently carry it outside. Then I vacuum up the web, which makes me feel very sad, but I do it anyway because I want the house to be clean for our guests. But I trust that this strong and savvy spider is going to try again. It's not going to give up and starve to death and it's not going to change its approach and start hunting for food. It will follow its instincts and find a new place to build an even bigger and better web than before.

So, when life tears down your dreams and destroys your hard work, don't give up and settle for something that feels difficult. Don't starve to death waiting for things to fix themselves. Be like the spider and trust that you're on the right path and that you have everything you need to survive and thrive. It doesn't matter how many times somebody comes along and knocks down your web or the wind blows and you're forced to begin again.

Trust your gut and do what feels right.

Keep going. Keep creating from the depths of your soul and you will *attract* everything you need to succeed.

Eventually, once this spider casts its new and even more immaculate web, what does it do next? It sits and waits patiently for food to come. It allows the Universe to handle the details. It allows nature to do its part to provide the food by staying still and trusting that all the delicious bugs it could ever need will fly into its web. The spider doesn't run around putting up webs in a bunch of different places. It stays put and waits for the flies to come. This is exactly how manifestation works! You're not meant to be creating all the time. Follow your intuition, take inspired action and then wait patiently to receive the rewards.

It's like if you were ordering a new couch for your living room. You wouldn't continue to sit at the computer after you made the purchase and keep clicking and reordering until your new couch arrived. You'd place the order. You'd get the confirmation email. You'd trust that it's on its way.

And what would you do next?

You'd probably sell or donate your old couch to make room for the new one, right? The biggest mistake I see people make when they're putting in their requests to the Universe is they hoard and hold onto what they have and fail to clear space for what they asked for because they're afraid that what they really want isn't coming.

Trust that the Universe has received your request. You don't have to keep thinking about it or checking back to make sure that the order went through. Get on with your life and make room for what you ordered. Soon enough, your new couch will arrive, and you can ask for something else. The key is spaciousness; release anything that conflicts with your desires and create space for them to manifest.

I found the following affirmations written in my journal:

"Magic resides in the space we create for it."

"The less I have, the more possibility."

"The less weight I'm carrying, the more capacity I have to receive all that's meant for me."

Imagine that everything you wanted was already on its way. Would you keep holding on to everything you have now? Take a moment to reflect on the space in your life and all that's filling it. Is there something you could drop to lighten the load? Do you have room for something new to manifest? If you received everything you've been calling in tomorrow, would you have the time and energy to nurture it? To enjoy it?

I went on to write, "And if you're not sure what you want, but you do know what you don't want, let go of all that doesn't feel good and make the space for better things to come along."

So what if you're not sure what to order next? Maybe you're overwhelmed by all the choices.

Chapter 9

It's like you're sitting in front of the TV, scrolling through Netflix, and you can't decide what to watch. You could spend hours looking through the options and reading the descriptions, but nothing is ever going to play unless you make a choice. Eventually, you choose something and maybe you love it!! But maybe you get about thirty minutes in, and you realize you picked a bad movie.

No big deal, right? You just exit back to the menu and choose again.

But when it comes to life, we're afraid to change our minds. We get deeply invested in things we don't even like, because we feel like it's too late to back out.

Or maybe you're stuck on the home screen, failing to try anything because you're afraid to make the wrong decision. But you don't have to overthink it. You can always change your mind later. Likewise, the world is full of infinite possibilities—more than you'll ever find on any streaming network. Don't waste a bunch of time stuck in a movie you hate or worse, staring at a screen with nothing playing because you're too afraid to pick something you might not like.

There will always be room for adjustments.

If you want to get better at making decisions on command, practice trusting your intuition.

When you can connect more confidently to your intuition, your decisions will become easier.

Like the spider who just knows exactly what to do when it's hungry, you too can listen for divine callings. You don't have to think so hard! Go with the flow and trust in yourself to know what's best for you.

We always have access to our intuitive nature, but often the voice of our mind interferes. All the noise we're constantly surrounded by gets in the way and makes it difficult to hear what that intuitive voice is telling us.

So, if you're feeling distracted or overwhelmed by all the choices and you're not sure what to do, step away from the hustle and bustle, slow down and tune into your inner wisdom by pulling an oracle card or closing your eyes and focusing on your heart space.

Here's a simple meditation exercise you can try when you're in need of some intuitive guidance from your highest self.

A Practice for Connecting to Your Highest Self

Find a comfortable seat and close your eyes.

Focus on relaxing every muscle in your body from the top of your head to the tips of your toes.

Take three, deep cleansing breaths. Release anything that isn't serving you at this moment and then return to a natural rhythm of breathing as you relax into your seat.

Bring your attention inward, noticing your heartbeat. Maybe you bring one hand to your heart and one to your belly, feeling the warmth of your body.

Visualize a flame or a warm, white light in your heart space. Think of this light as your spirit. It's always been there. It never burns out. It is always available to you.

Chapter 9

Imagine the warm light of your spirit circulating throughout your entire body. Feel it expand and fill you up until you're overflowing, and it starts to spill out, surrounding you and filling your space. Notice as it seeps out into the world, filling the entire Universe with light and love, guiding you and supporting you at all times.

Take one final, deep, loving breath in and out as you come back into your body, starting to wiggle your fingers and toes.

Notice how you feel.

When you're ready, open your eyes and say the following words aloud or in your mind's eye:

> *Surrounded by eternal light*
> *Filled with breath that gives me life*
> *I call the one who dwells inside*
> *Lead me forward, be my guide*
> *Sprinkle signs along my path*
> *Be my compass, be my map*
> *Ignite the flame inside my heart*
> *Show me where I need to start*
> *Pull me with my hearts desire*
> *Lift me up, when I tire*
> *Unlock the power I've stored within*
> *Earth, water, fire and wind*
> *Lead me where I need to go*
> *All I do is done in flow*

I find I don't need to be in silence or sitting in a meditation pose to connect with my intuition. I drop in most easily at art and music festivals. Here's a quick story to paint the picture of what it feels like when I'm channeling my highest self:

> *It was the second day of Austin City Limits, a three-day long music festival at Zilker Park in Austin, Texas. Our friend Mike was set on seeing his buddy, Chris, perform at 2:00 p.m. You probably know Chris from the classic movie Superbad. My husband, Alex, and I were down to see McLovin' play some bass, so we got to the festival early and followed Mike up to the front of the stage.*
>
> *I'd been off the sauce already for six months and knew that if I could make it through a festival weekend with my wildest friends without alcohol, that I had successfully broken my drinking habit. Cannabis would have been cool, but since we flew to Austin and couldn't bring it on the plane, I surrendered and figured it would come to me somewhere along the way if it were meant to be. The year before, I manifested a few giant joints that someone dropped on the ground and a lighter a few moments later!*

Magical moments like this are the norm at festivals—I think it's because the music opens my heart to the magic all around—but I guarantee if you start to pay attention and stay present in your daily life, you'll notice that it's happening all the time!

Everything you need will come to you when you're present and open.

Chapter 9

We're up at the front of the stage standing directly in front of Ben Kweller and Chris Mintz-Plasse, aka McLovin, and they're absolutely killing it. It's a gorgeously hot day and we'd forgotten our refillable water bottle at the house, but just when we got thirsty, the volunteer staff started passing out cartons of water and tossed a few straight to us! We quenched our thirst as we danced and enjoyed the show from the front row. A few songs in, a sweet couple next to us lit up a joint and passed it over. I gave them a bracelet in exchange for the hits and we bonded over our love for this feeling.[14]

The rest of the show was an emotional roller coaster. I'd tuned into the energy of the music and the crowd and every note, every word, and every feeling intensified. I cried tears of joy for the next hour or so, as I connected with the music and the voice of my highest self that always sings so clearly when I'm high on life. I felt a deep desire to communicate everything I knew to be true at that moment.

I am one with all there is!

I felt as if everything I could ever possibly need would be available to me—like I would never have to do it on my own again. I felt a sense of love and support from the Universe, effortlessly and innately in harmony with its divine organizing power! I was in awe of my own power and reminded of my purpose, as I was the year before during a sunset showstopper by Lil Nas X at the same festival:

I am meant to help people discover the magic that dwells inside their hearts.

I promise you don't need weed or live music to channel divine guidance. Sometimes I get this same sense of clarity while I'm

---

14. If you want more information on plant medicine and micro-dosing, please visit ShannonTheGoodWitch.com/TheHealthyHigh.

dancing alone around my apartment to a funky Spotify playlist or while I'm lying in the grass, basking in the sunshine, breathing in the world around me and relishing in the presence of God.

The inspired ideas inside of this book came to me in the form of what I like to call "high thoughts," or "downloads." It was an epiphany or a revelation of sorts. When I sat down to write, I tapped into my divine creative nature and the words simply poured into me. I was so full of enlightened information that I had no choice but to let it flow out. Had I kept it all in, I may have exploded.

So, I began to write.

The Healthy High is a compilation of my most recent understanding of the research in all things magic and manifestation and years of channeled wisdom.[15]

You, too, can "channel."

When you carve out time to dream, you'll find that it's easier than you think!

Have you ever had an epiphany (an illuminating discovery or profound sense of clarity)?

You can practice channeling divine downloads or "high thoughts" anywhere, anytime! Let the acronym H.I.G.H. guide you.

Maybe you try the following practice while sitting with your journal:

Channeling H.I.G.H. Thoughts

Help. Intention. Gratitude. Hope

---

[15] Visit ShannonTheGoodWitch.com/TheHealthyHigh for all my favorite books, podcasts, and educational resources on manifestation.

1. **Ask for Help:** You are one with all there is and you are always connected to the infinite, unbounded Universal force that makes up everything. The voice of your intuition is always speaking. Your angels and spirit guides are always communicating with you, so this first part of the ritual is about acknowledging their presence and opening your heart to receive divine messages. All you have to do is listen. Simply close your eyes, connect to your heart space, and ask your highest self for guidance before opening your journal for free flow writing.

2. **Set an Intention:** Once you've opened the portal by acknowledging your guides and asking for help, set a clear intention for your journaling practice. What messages are you hoping to receive? Maybe you're navigating an important decision and you want to explore the best possible outcome. Maybe you're feeling blocked and you're seeking inspiration. Affirm your aim for this channeling practice by writing it down. Form an open ended question or simply write "my highest self wants me to know. . . " and then freely write whatever comes through without hesitation. Allow your pen and paper to serve as a conduit for the messages of your soul.

3. **Offer Gratitude:** Give thanks for the information that comes through and trust that it's what you're meant to hear. Maybe you write a gratitude list in your journal or simply pause throughout your practice and into the day ahead to appreciate pleasant thoughts, fond memories, inspired ideas, new insights, and moments of clarity when you receive them.

The Healthy High

4 Express Hope: Close out your journaling practice by reflecting on your intention. Did you receive an answer to your prayers? Is there some newfound sense of hopefulness in your heart over a particular situation? What will you do with the divine downloads you received? What will you carry forward from this channeling session and how would you love that to impact your future? If you're still seeking clarity, express faith in your guides to show you the way when the time is right.

If you don't have your journal handy, or any scratch paper lying around, you can type what comes through or simply meditate on the four simple steps of this practice while you're walking through nature, dancing at a festival, or lying down to sleep at night.

Here's a list of things you can try to connect with your intuition:

Gardening	Dancing	Skipping
Painting	Journaling	Playing an instrument
Drawing	Singing	Listening to music
Walking	Reading	Scrapbooking
Yoga	Cooking	Stargazing
Swimming	Cleaning	Photography
Hiking	Organizing	Spellwork
Baking	Puppeteering	Building sandcastles
Flower picking	Pottery	Talking to your plants
Sunbathing	Driving	Gazing out the window
Crocheting	Running	Watching the clouds

I think you catch my drift—it could be anything! Maybe you're a digital creator and you love making Instagram reels or something like that. Do what feels good to you! Think back to some of the things that you did when you were a kid, like finger painting, chasing lightning bugs, or climbing trees. Try anything that helps you tap into your creativity and give yourself permission to get curious and play.

What if you had a list of mantras next to your bathroom mirror so that you're reminded to repeat them every time you wash your hands? You could even keep your favorite Tarot card deck on your nightstand, so that you can pull a card to help you reflect each night before bed.

Just like in my story about learning to play *The Entertainer* on the piano as a kid, muscle memory is real, and practice makes progress. In the same way, all our daily practices become our habits when we repeat them consistently over a period. Eventually, the new rituals you create will become an automatic part of your routine, so be intentional and incorporate fun activities that lift your spirits and raise your vibrations.[16]

To sum up what we've talked about in this chapter, I've listed out four simple steps to consider when you're manifesting anything.

1. Acknowledge your power.
2. Ask for what you want.
3. Act as if it's coming.
4. Appreciate whatever comes.

Notice that I used the word "appreciate" rather than "accept" for the final step. I don't want you settling for your circumstances, but I do want you to remember that manifestation is a cyclical practice.

---

16. Sign up for my 7-day Resolution Reset challenge at ShannonTheGoodWitch.com/links for a week's worth of actionable emails designed to help you build habits that stick.

You won't just do it once. Repeat these steps as you continue to manifest more and more of what you truly desire.

Our minds are so limited in comparison to the infinite, unbounded, expansive, creative potential available to us. Often, our brains can't even fathom what's possible and it can be difficult to see that there's better than what we've been chasing.

So, if there's something that you're calling in and you feel like it's not happening, trust that there's a reason and that it will all play out in divine timing or that something better is coming along. Be patient and keep an open mind.

Life will inevitably throw you hard balls out of left field. Practice reading the signs, give it your best shot and take it play by play. My Pap would say, "You can't win 'em all." Playing isn't about winning. It's about having fun and improving your skills with every game!

Here's a simple acronym I find helpful when I'm building a P.R.A.C.T.I.C.E. of anything:

P.R.A.C.T.I.C.E. Makes Progress.
Play. Rest. Ask. Contemplate. Try. Incorporate. Clean. Elevate.

Play: Have fun with it! There's no right or wrong here. Get curious and enjoy the process.

Rest: Take routine breaks. If you were training for a marathon, you wouldn't run all day, every day. You'd start with a mile or two and work your way up with each run. In between, you'd give your legs time to recover. It's important to rest your mind and body so that you can come back stronger, time and time again.

Ask: Request some guidance from an expert. Maybe you find a free YouTube video, take a class or you hire a coach. Watch, learn and don't be afraid to ask for help when you need it. Recruit some accountability to keep you on track.

Contemplate: Reflect on your trial and error. What went well and what felt difficult? Build a habit of checking in and tracking your growth.

Try: Give it your best shot! Think of anything you're practicing as an experiment. You'll improve as you go.

Incorporate: How can you incorporate your new practice into your daily life in a way that sticks? When I'm working to form a new habit, I find it helpful to build on existing habits. For example, maybe you're working on your writing skills. What if every time you opened your laptop to check your email in the morning, you dedicated five minutes to creative writing? You're already sitting down at your computer! Simply set a timer and let the ideas flow before you open your inbox.

Clean: When you're practicing anything, don't be afraid to color outside of the lines. You can go back in and clean up what you've created. With every pass at it, you'll get a little more precise, but have fun and don't be afraid to get messy. Make a mess, clean up later!

Elevate: This part happens naturally. The more you try, the better you'll become at whatever it is that you're practicing. Give yourself grace, learn from your mistakes and continue moving your way up the ladder one step at a time.

Pause for a moment to consider some steps that you can take to practice connecting to your intuition more regularly. Is there a particular activity from the list I shared a few pages back that caught your attention? Maybe there's something you used to do for fun that you'd like to revisit. Make a list of three or four practices that you're excited to try. Circle one that you're going to do this week and schedule it into your calendar!

When I'm practicing *Yoga with Adriene* on YouTube, my teacher, Adriene Mishler says to "find what feels good." It's not about doing things perfectly or following her instructions to the letter. She teaches us to modify and cater to our own needs. We're all different and we can't expect that the same practices are going to work for everyone.[17] Move through these lessons like you're at a buffet. Take what resonates with you and leave the rest. This is your journey, after all. You are in the driver's seat!

In Chapter Ten: Manifesting with the Moon, I'm sharing my discovery of the Lunar Phases and how syncing up with them has changed my life for the better!

---

17. Be sure to visit ShannonTheGoodWitch.com/TheHealthyHigh to unlock a heap of supporting resources and recommendations to help you manifest your most ecstatic life.

CHAPTER 10

Manifesting with the Moon

It was a warm day in Salem, Massachusetts in July 2021, when Alex and I parked for a spontaneous pitstop on our way to Old Orchard Beach, Maine where we had a motel room waiting for us. The whole trip was spontaneous since we'd traded it for the three-week tour of Italy and Paris we'd originally planned for our honeymoon the year before, but we drove off to the East Coast in the heat of Summer, ready to make the best of our delayed celebration. In all the chaos of planning and replanning our wedding during a global pandemic, **we accidentally booked our first Airbnb in Rhode Island for just one** night instead of two, leaving us to make last-minute arrangements for our second night away. We had friends in Boston and decided to spend the night at a cute boutique hotel in the Little Italy District. (I guess we got a taste of Roma after all!) During an evening out eating, dancing, and drinking espresso, we were encouraged to explore some shops in Salem along the journey to the beach.

When I entered *Haus Witch*, a sense of wonder sent chills down my spine and a burst of serotonin flooded my veins. I'm sure

I resembled a kid in a candy shop. Suddenly all the mix-ups seemed fortuitous—like I was meant to be there. I picked up a book called *Haus Magick* by Erica Feldmann and flipped through the pages. I noticed a photo of the author printed inside and when I looked up, there she was, standing behind the counter. Seeing this woman who'd written this magical book and created this brick and mortar storefront full of candles and crystals that were speaking so loudly to me had me mesmerized. I admired her craftsmanship and saw myself in her—a good witch with a desire to spread love. I picked up a few more items, including a manifestation spell kit to give to my mom who'd been on the hunt for a new place to live. (Spoiler alert: we performed the spell and she found her dream apartment the next day!) Anyhow, I finally got to reading my new favorite book once we made it to the beach and my love affair with the Moon began.

In the lunar phases, I recognized my own infradian rhythm as a menstruator who operates on a twenty-eight-day hormonal carnival ride, and loved this reminder that I'm a cyclical being. Seven months earlier, I was listening to an episode of *The Goal Digger Podcast* with Jenna Kutcher and Kate Northrup when I discovered that I had been suppressing my natural cycle for eleven years with the birth control pill.[18] When I found out the pill was shutting down my entire hormonal system, I was angry. I was angry with my doctors, but angrier with myself for failing to do the research. I immediately stopped taking the pill that I'd been prescribed at the age of sixteen and signed up for a course to learn about my body. I made it my priority to turn my secondary clock into a superpower and decided that I would no longer suppress my feminine gifts—I would lean into them.

---

18. Head to ShannonTheGoodWitch.com/Moon for a link to the episode and more resources!

Chapter 10

The symbolism I'd discovered in this new way of looking at my body and the Moon resonated with me. It reminded me of my manifestation practice and gave me a direct and easy plan to incorporate it into my daily life. Now, I look to the changing faces of the Moon for guidance when I'm manifesting anything and simultaneously appreciate the reminder to honor my dynamic energy levels. Since then, I've learned to create more ease in my daily life by syncing up with the lunar calendar and the fluctuations of my hormones. I conquered my belief that I needed to show up and hustle every single day that the sun rises and falls like we're taught to do in this masculine driven world.

What if we learned to honor our seasonal nature? Not just as women, but as a society. Long before we had the modern-day calendar, the Moon's cyclical nature helped people tell time and plan their activities. Research shows that people have been looking to the seasons and the sky for guidance for more than thirty-thousand years. It serves as a daily reminder to honor the ebbs and flows of our natural energy levels.

Here are some facts you should know about the Moon before we get into the symbolism.

According to NASA, the moon exerts a strong gravitational pull that causes the changing tides in our bodies of water and regulates the climate of the Earth, making it a livable planet. We always see the same side of the Moon, because as it revolves around Earth, it also rotates, causing the same side to always face us. The moon looks different every night because the Moon orbits the earth while the Earth orbits the sun. Everything is moving.

The moonlight we see on Earth is sunlight reflected off the Moon's surface. The amount of Moon we see illuminated changes over the month. When sunlight is lighting only the Moon's near side—the side that always faces Earth—we see a Full Moon. When sunlight illuminates just the far side of the Moon, it appears to be dark, and we call it a New Moon. The rest of the month, we see a different amount of the daytime side of the Moon each night. These continually changing views of the sunlit part of the Moon are the Moon's phases.

When the moon goes dark, we mark the beginning of a new twenty-nine-and-a-half-day lunar cycle. After a brief period of darkness, the moon grows in appearance for about two weeks until the next Full Moon. Around day fifteen of the lunar cycle, the moon reaches peak illumination and will appear full and bright in the sky. For about two weeks after peak illumination, the moon begins to shrink in appearance until the next New Moon.

For now, here are the four lunar phases you need to know for manifestation:

The Full Moon—a symbolic summer season—a time to CELEBRATE your harvest

A Full Moon is a reminder to give thanks for the abundance already present in your life. It is a time to harvest the fruits of your labor and to collect the rewards from the accumulated action you've taken to cultivate your "garden of life." It's a time to gather and share your feast. Give thanks for your meal and dig in! This is a time to ground down and tune into the rhythms of the Universe with dancing, singing and celebration! Find the pleasure in being alive.

Chapter 10

The Waning Moon—a symbolic autumn season—a time to CLEAR space for new growth

The Waning Moon is a symbol for letting go and releasing. It is a time to drop the extra weight you've been carrying like a tree in fall, shedding its leaves to preserve energy for the winter season ahead. I like to use the mark of the Last Quarter Moon as a reminder to reflect on my progress, tidy up my spaces, and tie up loose ends on any outstanding projects. It's time to get things done, like an animal busy preparing for hibernation. Focus on donating or recycling anything that's not serving you physically or energetically and think about making room for something better to come along.

The New Moon—a symbolic winter season—a time to CONNECT to your divine nature

The New Moon, also called the Dark Moon, is the mark of a new lunar cycle and a time to welcome in a fresh start. The New Moon serves as a symbolic New Year and recognition of a new beginning. Use this time to reflect, recharge, and reset. Spend some quiet time away from your community and connect to the voice of your highest self.

The Waxing Moon—a symbolic spring season—a time to CULTIVATE your dream life

I like to use the First Quarter Moon as a marker for shifting my focus to the creation phase of my manifestation practice. A Waxing Moon symbolizes amplification, growth and expansion. It's a good time to take inspired action toward your goals. The growing energy of the Waxing Moon will aid in your progress. Think of this like the springtime when you're tending to your garden, planting and watering the seeds of your inspired ideas.

Cyclical patterns play out through nature. Our bodies follow circadian and infradian rhythms, the earth rotates and revolves around the sun, and plants and animals hibernate through winter. Women often correlate their menstrual cycle to the lunar calendar and notice that maybe they bleed every month near the New Moon and ovulate with the Full Moon or vice versa. Just like the four main phases of the lunar cycle, the four phases of the female hormonal cycle can be compared to the seasons. The Menstrual Phase is like a winter season, the Follicular Phase is like a spring season, the Ovulatory Phase is like a summer season, and the Luteal Phase is like an autumn season.

The Female Hormonal Cycle and the Moon

Ovulation Phase—a symbolic summer season

The Ovulatory Phase is like summer and can be a great time for socializing and nurturing your community. If I were comparing ovulation to the lunar phases, it would be like the Full Moon. During ovulation, hormone levels rise to their peak. It's a time of the cycle when women are said to be glowing! The boost in hormones might give them a boost in energy, just like the powerful energy of the Full Moon does, so it's safe to push limits here and exert extra energy where it counts.

Luteal Phase—a symbolic autumn season

The Waning Moon Phase can be compared to the Luteal Phase of the female hormonal cycle, also known as the PMS phase. Progesterone, also known as the "keep calm, carry on hormone," rises during the Luteal Phase. This is a good time for menstruators to spend away from their communities taking care of their personal responsibilities and preparing to take a rest during their upcoming periods. The metabolism will start to speed up during this phase, so a boost in healthy snacks and lighter workouts are welcome here. Keep in mind though that sugar, carbs, caffeine, and alcohol could intensify PMS symptoms.

Menstrual Phase—a symbolic winter season
We can compare the Menstrual Phase of the female hormonal cycle to the New Moon phase of the lunar cycle. Women should carve out extra time for rest, reflecting and nourishing their bodies while they're bleeding, and their hormone levels are at their lowest. Nature walks and stretching are healthy ways to move without overdoing it. Women will likely feel more in tune with their intuition during the menstrual phase. The right and left hemispheres of the brain work cohesively during this period, so it's a good time for contemplation and decision making.

Follicular Phase—a symbolic spring season
The Follicular Phase of the female hormonal cycle can be compared to the Waxing Moon Phase, when energy levels are on the rise. Often, women report feeling more creative during this time of the month. The emotional brain turns off and allows the mind to freely focus on strategic planning. This is a great week for women to take inspired action, hit the weights at the gym or pick up the pace in their workouts.

I would love to note that just because we've compared the Menstrual Phase to the New Moon Phase, and Ovulation to the Full Moon, doesn't mean that menstruators will always bleed with the New Moon and ovulate with the Full Moon. Every person is different, so make a point to notice and track your bodily functions and honor your health above all else.[19]

My life has transformed since quitting the birth control pill and making more informed choices for my body. I wouldn't suggest dropping a prescribed medication before talking to your doctor like I did, but I couldn't wrap up this chapter without mentioning the overall improvement I've noticed in my health. It took about a year to balance out my hormones, but now, my I have pain-free, predictable periods. I don't get terrible cramps or experience any breast tenderness like I used to, unless I've overdone it on caffeine or sweets during my luteal phase. I haven't had a cold sore or suffered from an illness since 2020. I still breakout and my flow is certainly heavier now that I'm having a real period instead of the spotting I'd experience during my sugar pill week when my body was withdrawing from the medication, but I feel happier, healthier, and more empowered overall now that I honor the phases of my cycle.

Thanks to a digital course called *Power of Periodization* with the Balanced Beyars Sisters, a book called *In the Flo* by Alisa Vitti, and all the women normalizing period talk around the world, I feel more in tune with my body than I've ever felt before. I celebrate my period and the intuitive powers that come along with it! I block off rest days while I'm bleeding so that I can rest, reflect and channel divine wisdom. The changing phases of my female hormonal cycle have

---

19. You can find a printable Lunar Planner to track your cycle and set your intentions around the moon markers along with all my favorite resources for menstruators and moonbeams at ShannonTheGoodWitch.com/Moon.

become my greatest superpower. I want to help you harness yours too.

My lunar manifestation ritual isn't just designed for women. All of us earthly beings are a part of nature and can benefit from adopting a lunar lifestyle. The moon is available to everyone, and if it's energy effects the earth, it must affect us too.

Aligning your actions with the lunar phases is a fun and easy way to create anything you could possibly dream for your life. Now that you've got a basic understanding of what I mean when I say, "manifesting with the moon" feel free to start implementing what you've learned right away.[20]

The following four chapters are devoted to the individual phases of my lunar manifestation ritual. Each chapter begins with a personal anecdote and concludes with practical guidance for each phase of the lunar cycle, so that you can walk away from this book with a lasting habit of nurturing your spiritual growth.

In Chapter Eleven: Celebrate your Harvest with the Full Moon, I'll begin with a recent story about holding on to hope through hardship, and then, tie it all together with actionable steps for the Full Moon phase.

When you're ready, take your seat and buckle up for a ride on the Moonbeam Express!

---

[20]. Head to ShannonTheGoodWitch.com/Moon to download my digital Manifesting with the Moon Guidebook. Inside, you'll find a visual representation of the Lunar Cycle and actionable tips for each phase.

CHAPTER 11
Celebrate Your Harvest with The Full Moon

When I lost my dad unexpectedly in February 2024, Alex and I were preparing to leave for another trip to Costa Rica, but after my dad's passing, I felt unsure about traveling. Our original plans to stay at a friend's new surf camp fell through because the business closed just short of our arrival. We considered canceling, but our flights were non-refundable, so we booked a last-minute stay in La Fortuna—a part of the country we hadn't been before—and decided the time in nature would be healing.

The week before the trip was tough. As my dad's only child, the responsibilities of cleaning out his apartment and locating his important documents fell to me. Even though sorting through his belongings scared me, it felt good to be there in his presence. The way he made lists and saved return addresses by tearing off the corners of envelopes made me realize all the things we had in common. I saw myself in him. Finding the cards I sent him and photos of us made me happy; and seeing how organized and tidy he kept everything brought me peace. I always worried he was lonely living there on his own, but I like to think he enjoyed his solitude and independence in those final years of his life.

The day before we learned he passed, I said I could really go for some of my dad's chili. Low and behold, he had a couple of containers saved in the freezer. On the night before we left for Costa Rica, we heated it up and had it for dinner. It was just as delicious as I remembered. My heart and belly felt full as I sobbed through a smile. I knew he wouldn't want me to cancel our flights and throw away nine hundred dollars. He'd want us to go and have a good time. Knowing that his spirit lives on in my heart gave me even more reason to go. I wanted him to experience the beauty of Costa Rica too.

It turns out, getting away with Alex in such a serene place for a long weekend was just what I needed. As we sat at the Liberia airport waiting for our flight home, I contemplated the complexity of human emotion. How can it be possible to feel sad and joyful all at once? I'm not sure I have an answer for you, but from my experience, I can tell you it is possible. Feelings aren't black and white. They're vibrant and colorful like a rainbow. You're not crazy for crying one moment and laughing the next. Feel it all! There's beauty to be discovered in the pain, and meaning to be found in the difficult times.

Death is inevitable, life goes on. Let's make the best of it while we're here.

Focus on anything that brings you joy and find the good in even the shittiest circumstances, because someday you'll find a message in the mess and you'll see the meaning behind the madness. Celebrate this season and give thanks for it, because it's a part of your story and someday could be the cornerstone of your best-selling book.

Seek out simple ways to make your days a little more magical, like smelling flowers, wishing on dandelions, and smiling at strangers.

What are you celebrating in this season of life? Make a list of all you're grateful for, starting with simple things like your body and your breath. Maybe you are currently going through something that feels like a challenge. What can you learn from it? Everything is an opportunity for growth and for reflection.

Here's a mantra I say to relieve anxiety during stressful situations:

A Mantra for Cultivating Trust in a Higher Power

Everything is as it should be
The Universe is working for me

In magical practices, the Full Moon symbolizes abundance and gratitude. It's a time for welcoming positivity into your life and a reminder to give thanks.

You might feel a heightened sense of energy during a Full Moon, so lean into your power, shine your radiant light for all to see, and gather with people who lift your spirits.

Take that Full Moon energy into the first few days of the Waning Moon and indulge in every delicious, delectable piece of the divine life unfolding before you. Dig in and seize the day. Take inspired action and say yes to the opportunities that feel aligned. Tomorrow isn't promised, so eat like it's your last meal, dance like no one's watching, and share what you've got with the people you love. Don't worry about saving some for later.

Here's a memory I often reference to help me shift from a scarcity mindset to an abundance mindset:

I was having dinner with Alex, our friend's Mike and Kaylah, and some of their pals in New York City. We were sitting at one of their favorite restaurants, sharing a bunch of appetizers, and I was holding back on finishing up the arancini when Kaylah invited me to take the last one. Something she said stuck with me. Matter of factly, she simply stated, "We can always order more." She was right. Yes, we absolutely could have ordered more at any point!

I wondered how often I had been doing this in my life. Had I been holding back and saving some for later because I had a fear of running out or didn't want to take from someone else?

When you're putting in your request to the Universe, remember that there's plenty to go around.

There will always be enough for everyone, so take what you want and leave what you don't.

Think of your desires like running water. There's an endless supply flowing freely out of the faucet to fill your cup full. Don't be afraid to drink up! There's always going to be more where that came from!

Three Actionable Steps for The Full Moon: A Symbolic Summer Season and a Time to Celebrate Your Harvest

1. Deliver: In those final days of the Waxing Moon phase, when the Moon is almost full, it's a great time to crush your to-do list. Use that extra energy to show up for yourself. Holding yourself accountable and following through on your promises builds confidence. Plus, you'll feel ready to celebrate and let loose if you've already accomplished a task. Remember, done is better than perfect. Do what you can and then take a well-deserved break.

2. Dance: You are on a journey of divine transformation. Before you close the door on one chapter and step forward into the next, find what you love about each season of life and soak it up. Enjoy the heck out of it. Say yes to aligned opportunities, give thanks for every experience, and don't be afraid to try something new! Express yourself and gather with people that love you for you. Try activities that help you find pleasure in ordinary moments and celebrate your symbolic harvest.

3. Devour: During a Full Moon and the days to follow, give thanks for your symbolic harvest. Dig in and share! Don't hold back! Don't worry about running out. There's always going to be more where that came from.

One last thing to mention about the Full Moon phase...

Sometimes, I notice Full Moon energy feels overwhelming and might not have me wanting to go out and celebrate. You don't have to physically throw a party, but let the bright moon remind you to take inventory of the abundance all around you.

Maybe you feel like you've outgrown your life. The grass might be greener on the other side, but don't get so caught up longing for something different that you miss out on all the magic that's present where you are now.

Just to be clear, you don't have to stop practicing gratitude after the Full Moon. I simply like to use the Full Moon as a signal to celebrate and raise my vibrations, but the tips and tricks I share for every phase of the lunar cycle, can be applied anytime.

Before we move into the next phase of the ritual, I'll leave you with a trick I use to help me seize the days.

I'm an avid listener of the Jay Shetty podcast, *On Purpose*. If you know the show, you know that at the end of every interview, he asks his guests a set of rapid-fire questions. One of those questions is, "What's the best advice you have ever received?" So, I thought about this for myself and quickly concluded that the best advice I had ever received was from my mom in the form of our song, *I Hope You Dance* by LeeAnne Womack. These lyrics pretty much sum it up–

"When you get the choice to sit it out or dance, I hope you dance."

By my mom's example, I've learned to dance through life, seizing the day and making the most of the resources available to me. There's a rhythm to the Universe, and if you want to sync up with it, you've gotta be willing to D.A.N.C.E.

Use this acronym to help:

I Hope You D.A.N.C.E.

Desire. Allow. Notice. Collaborate. Express.

Desire: Trust that your desires are leading you to the fulfillment of your dharma. Follow them like breadcrumbs from your highest self who knows exactly what to do at all times!

Allow: What if you allowed yourself to explore your curiosities? We tend to suppress our desires for the sake of fitting in or keeping up with our daily responsibilities. We put off the things we really want to do because we don't feel worthy, or because we're afraid of what people will think. Give yourself permission to lead with your heart. Do what feels right.

Notice: Pay attention to what you're daydreaming about. What's on your heart? Is there something sparking your interest or pulling you in a particular direction? Are you being guided to a particular person or place in the world, or maybe toward a new activity you'd like to try or an event you'd love to attend? Keep a journal to note your thoughts!

Collaborate: Ask for help and co-create with your peers. There's no need to do it alone. There's so much magic that comes from working with the world around you. How can you use the people and assets in your arena to create something beautiful? I owe my success to all the other artists who've helped me along the way. When I started my wedding videography business, I brought in drone pilots and second shooters that had talents that complemented mine! Together, we were able to create something more beautiful and professional that I couldn't have created on my own and I got to learn from them along the way. Explore new relationships and join forces with other creatives, especially the ones who inspire and celebrate you. Offer your services when you can and phone a friend when you need help.

Express: The more you share yourself and your ideas with the people around you, the easier it's going to be to attract a tribe to lift you up and cheer you on! Wear your heart on your sleeve and don't be afraid to let that freak flag fly. It's like carrying a big rainbow totem around the festival to call in your friends. Your totem isn't just going to help you stay close to the group you arrived with. It's going to attract new people who resonate with it. Express yourself freely and play with the people you're attracting.

Be kind, do your best, enjoy the little things, and seize the freakin' day because you never know how much time you, or the people you love, have left. Romanticize the crap out of your life because you deserve the best.

List out a few ways you're going to invite more magic into your life on a daily basis.

In Chapter Twelve: Clear The Way for New Growth with The Waning Moon, you'll learn why it's necessary to prune your plants if you want to create an abundant garden that's not overgrown with weeds. I'm sharing an epiphany that showed me that my desires weren't manifesting, because my life was full of clutter. If you're ready to turn your messes into magic and make room for all the blessings coming your way, keep reading!

CHAPTER 12

Clear The Way for New Growth with The Waning Moon

The Waning Moon Phase is a time to take *aligned* action toward your personal goals. During this phase, carve out time to tidy up your life and release anything that's weighing you down. Let the Last Quarter Moon marker serve as your reminder to let go of anything that's not serving your highest good.

Take a beat to reflect:

What's eating up your time and energy? What's preventing you from taking the necessary steps to get from where you are now to where you want to go? Is there someone or something in your day-to-day life leaving you feeling drained and burned out?

I'm not sure of the exact moment it happened—this decision had been a long time coming— but sometime around the new year, heading into 2024, I decided that I would no longer make a living trading my time for money. I'd known for years that I had the capacity to make a global impact sharing my story and my perspective through a book, but I hadn't committed to it. There were always things getting in the way, keeping me small and preventing me from pursuing what I'd always felt called to do.

I started writing this book in 2015 while I was still working in news, but when I did finally get the courage to leave behind my career in pursuit of something that felt more fulfilling, I got caught up in life. I was enjoying my freedom. I was still writing and brainstorming subtitles, but I'd never set a real goal to finish a first draft so I allowed all the other ways I was making money and having fun to take priority.

I loved serving and bartending. I got to hangout and lift people's spirits as I delivered their drinks and meals. I got to network and nurture my community and I'd take home wads of cash every single shift. Writing wasn't paying my bills yet. I couldn't write and simultaneously spend time with my friends who I'd missed so much while I was stuck at a news station in West Virginia, working the night shift. But I could bring my camera and tell stories and make connections through the art of film and photography.

That's when people started asking me to document their big life events and milestones. So when I was presented with this new stream of income doing something that I was already doing for fun, how could I say no? Over the next several years, my business grew quickly. I'd turned my hobby into a cash flow generating business and I was having a blast along the way! I felt successful and financially independent. I liked that feeling. I liked being able to provide for myself, and I absolutely loved being a hype woman. But it took a ton of time and energy.

Chapter 12

I was constantly telling Alex that he should make YouTube videos teaching people about personal finance and wellness. I saw him as a natural born entertainer and a role model that people trusted and looked to for health and money advice. I encouraged him to make a guide or a course to sell online. I knew it was possible to create something once and sell it passively and I wanted to do it myself, but I didn't have the time.

I wasn't making the time.

With my spare moments away from shooting and editing, I was partying, and so was he. I wasn't committed to changing my business model because it wasn't that bad. He wasn't focused on growing his Tik Tok channel because he was comfortable with his eighty thousand dollar a year salary. He didn't like going to work, but it was a means to an end. He wanted to retire at forty with two million dollars that would pay dividends each year, and figured he could suck it up and settle for a less than satisfying career while he saved up to make it happen.

Me, on the other hand, I liked what I was doing! Wedding videography was rewarding. It was enjoyable. It was working. It made sense to people. My clients raved about me and recommended me to everyone. I loved receiving this kind of praise and recognition for my skills and my art. It was an ego boost and I let that keep me stuck in the grind longer than I should have.

Eventually, I hit a wall, and I knew that something had to shift. I was a perfectionist and a people pleaser and cared about making my clients happy at the expense of my own mental and physical health.

After a few years of overextending myself, I finally learned to set some boundaries with my clients. I'd written into my contracts that it could take up to eight months to deliver their wedding films, and they graciously understood (for the most part). I explained that I did all my shooting in the busy season and that I would catch up on my editing in the slower winter months.

But the problem was, I'd let my work pile up until the last minute, because I needed a winter season for rest.

Sometimes, when I wasn't working on a tight deadline, I'd start working on my book again or some other fun idea that sparked inspiration. But eventually the deadlines would approach, and I'd be forced to pause my passion projects and stay up all night finishing my videos and galleries. I hadn't learned to outsource. I didn't have a system in place that made it possible.

I was doing it all on my own.

Alex would always say, "Why pay someone to do it when you could do it yourself?" And for the longest time, I agreed with him. I felt confident in my skills and I wanted to do it all. So, I did. I believed that outsourcing would be more difficult than sitting down and busting out the editing myself.

I worked well under pressure. Sometimes it was the only way I could get anything done. I started telling my clients to expect their films on a certain day just so that I'd be forced to sit down and get the editing and blog posts finished. I'm a woman of my word so I knew that if I set a deadline for myself and shared that deadline with my clients, I would triumph. And that feeling of completion always felt amazing! But this cycle would repeat itself more than one hundred times until I finally retired from weddings and decided that there was another, better way.

Chapter 12

I could no longer set aside my health or my vision for helping millions of people around the world. I wanted more and this made me realize that I'd been working too hard for something that must not have been all that important to me.

As a multi-passionate person with a cup-half-full mentality, it can be very easy for me to fall into the trap of juggling all the things, but I've learned that if I want to have the time and energy for what's most important to me, that I'd have to start shedding some extra weight.

The success of my production company depended on things like the quality of my gear and editing software. I was constantly upgrading my equipment and adding new assets to my armory of cameras and lenses and microphones. There was no end in sight to the perpetual evolution of the tech industry, and if I wanted to stay relevant as a videographer, I needed to have the latest and greatest supplies and know how to use them. I was seeing the return on my investments, so the cost of my gear never bothered me and I loved paying my friends to second shoot or stand in for me when I was double booked.

What really started getting to me was the amount of lugging I was doing.

I was in the best shape of my life during those busy shooting seasons. Carrying around tripods and gimbals and heavy bags full of electronics was a workout! I always appreciated that it kept me fit because I'm not one for the gym. I was strong, I was toned, and I was proud of my guns. But I couldn't see myself running around in such a high stress environment, literally lugging baggage with me everywhere for the rest of my working life. When I really tuned into my heart's desire and called to mind the feelings that correlated, I felt light, I felt free, and I felt like I could fly! This lifestyle I'd created just didn't align anymore with where I was headed.

I started thinking of ways to lighten the load.

Eventually I recognized the clutter I'd collected in every area of my life. I started purging my spaces of all the stuff I was holding onto "just in case I might need it someday."

I'm no longer focused on how I can obtain more things, but instead, I'm focusing my attention on creating more space and I feel more peaceful and prosperous than ever before.

I don't want more gear to lug around, I don't want more commitments on my calendar, and I certainly don't want more work to do when I've got a life to live and people to love.

I simply want more magic, more freedom, and more simplicity.

Turns out, I don't have to own anything to be happy.

Now that Alex and I have both adopted this "less is more" mentality, we've made it our mission to let go of anything and everything that's been weighing us down. We want as little as possible holding us back from enjoying nature and traveling freely and spontaneously. We're focusing on how we can have enough cash flow to sustain our desire to see the world.

We don't need another house. We don't need another thirty-year mortgage. What if instead of thousands of dollars a month on interest, utilities, property taxes, and maintenance costs, we booked a short-term rental in a new place every season and collected experiences and memories rather than keepsakes and dust bunnies?

I'm tired of accumulating junk.

I don't have to have an outfit for every occasion. I can stop at a thrift store and pick up something to wear and donate anything that doesn't fit in my suitcase.

Chapter 12

I stopped highlighting my hair and wearing makeup so that I'm not wasting time keeping up with appearances. Sometimes I dress in athletic wear, others like a hippie festival chick with minimal clothing and glitter all over my body. Usually, I'm in my orange cargo pants with an old T-shirt I tie dyed, or my favorite purple sweater, but I'm an outfit repeater and keep a small wardrobe.

I even stopped carrying around my crystals and my lucky troll doll, Doug, because I've learned to tap into their energy from anywhere. I used to bring Doug all around the world in my backpack so that I could rub the gem on his belly for good fortune. My trolls and crystals give me a physical way to interact with my spirit guides, but I've learned that it's not necessary and just as powerful to close my eyes and pray.

A minimal lifestyle works for me. I'm more open to receiving because my days aren't full of chaos and clutter.

This is not to say that you can't or that you shouldn't own anything. We are all built with different desires. Your ideal of rich isn't going to look like anyone else's, which is exactly why there's plenty to go around for all of us. Manifestation expert, Katherine Zenkina says,

"What is desired by you is destined for you."

Getting rich isn't about keeping up with the Joneses. To be rich is to have all your desires easily met. It's about shifting from a scarcity mindset to an abundance mindset and remembering that everything you need is available. We're each ingrained with unique callings meant to lead us toward our purpose and bring the Universe into balance.

When it comes to my spaces, I can be a type A, Virgo, perfectionist. I'm neat and tidy and like things in their place. Organizing is my superpower.

My mom sits on the opposite end of the spectrum. She is the epitome of a girl's girl, and loves fashion, makeup, and jewelry. Her closets are jam-packed with clothing and shoes and purses of all colors, shapes and sizes. She collects things like recyclable bags from her daily trips to the drug store and buys duplicates of most items because she can never seem to find what she needs when she needs it.

This major difference in our preferences has caused us to butt heads over the years, especially when we were living together.

I always loved getting my hands on my mom's bedrooms and medicine cabinets. She feels better when she has a clean and tidy space and she's grateful for my help, but sometimes she takes my tidying personally and thinks I'm criticizing her messiness. I've had to learn to let go of my desire to clean up for her.

Now, I only organize when she asks for my help or I offer to dedicate a day, specifically for cleaning, while she's out and about so that she can come home to a cozy apartment.

This simple shift has healed our relationship.

The truth is, I was triggered by her mess, so I wanted to fix it. I've had to do a lot of personal work to get to a place where I don't react to triggers. I've learned that I can only control how I respond and that if I stay calm and display patience, people can't argue with me. I'm not saying I don't get frustrated or triggered. I most certainly do!

But I don't react.

I take a deep breath and let it go.

My mom might be disorganized, but she's a powerful manifestor in her own way. Instead of setting goals and planning, she simply asks for what she needs when she needs it, and it magically appears in divine timing.

Chapter 12

Sure, there were lots of times she felt tight on money, but she prayed her way through and gave credit to God when things worked out. She fell into job opportunities and manifested raises and bonuses that paid for my private piano lessons and her friends' rent payments when they needed help.

Because she's kind, generous, and serves people with *her* superpowers, the Universe rewards her.

I wasn't designed for the traditional nine to five grind, but my mom on the other hand, thrived in a typical working environment. (Picture Leslie Knope from *Parks and Recreation*, but all dolled up.) As a single mom, she craved stability and benefits, so she found a job she enjoyed that provided security for us. For 38 years, she excelled in her role with the Public Works Department of the City of Pittsburgh, managing hundreds of people who adored and respected her over the course of her career. If she ran for mayor, I believe she'd win with all the friendships she'd maintained throughout her lifetime.

At seventy-three years old, my mom finally retired so that she could have more energy for dancing on the weekends, planning events and presentations for one of the many organizations she's a part of, and socializing with friends. She's got better things to do than clean her apartment.

She's my hero and a role model to many.

Just as I manifested Alex, the perfect partner with gifts that compliment mine, my mom manifested me. I'm far from the perfect daughter, and we don't always see eye to eye, but my love for her sparks the drive in me to succeed. I dream so big and work so hard because I desire to take care of her, just as she took care of me all those years as a single mom.

As much as I like to think I'm a go with the flow kind of girl, I struggle to loosen my grip on the reins of my daily responsibilities. I desire to have an easier life than my mom had, and I want to be able to help people without struggling or sacrificing my own needs. I want the best for everyone, and I know the best is possible, so I've got high expectations for myself and others, but we're all on individual journeys.

Nowadays, I practice staying in my lane, focusing my energy toward becoming the best version of myself so I can help my loved ones when they need me.

The fact that my relationship with my mom looks like it does today, with very minimal arguing and mostly pleasant and loving interactions, lets me know that I'm doing something right. Now that I don't react, she's less reactive too. She drives me crazy sometimes, but she's my best friend and I'm grateful we're so close.

The things people say to us don't have to ruin our entire day. The annoyances don't have to turn into blow out arguments that last hours, weeks, or years on end. You don't have to forgive and forget, but you can forgive and move forward.

When people push your buttons, pop open the hood and figure out what's causing all the blinking red lights on the dash. It's important to stop for routine maintenance, just like you do with your car. You can only go on ignoring all the warning signs so long before you break down in the middle of the highway and you're forced to pull over and ask for help. So, when someone or something triggers you, slow down and take inventory of your surroundings. Pull over for a pit-stop, fill up the tank, give the windows a wash and check your tire pressure while you're at it. Set yourself up for success moving forward and do your best to prepare so that those minor potholes and nearby traffic accidents won't run you off the road. Pay attention. There's so much to learn about yourself when you hit a speed bump. How did you handle it?

What emotional baggage or deconstructive thoughts can you release? Is it anger? Resentment? Anxiety? Write it down to process and let go of any trapped traumas.

Three Actionable Steps for the Waning Moon Phase: A Symbolic Autumn Season and a Time to Clear the Way for New Growth

1. Deliberate: It's important to pause every so often to reflect on your progress. Let the Last Quarter Moon serve as your reminder to check in with your goals. You are constantly growing and changing, so it only makes sense that your goals would grow and change along with you. If you find that a goal you've been working toward doesn't quite line up with the feelings that you hoped to manifest in your life, PIVOT! It's okay to change your mind!

2. Delegate: You can do anything, but you can't do everything. If you're coming up with plans to accomplish high aspirations all on your own, you're bound to hit a point where you begin to feel overwhelmed or stuck. What keeps you up at night? If there's something that doesn't feel aligned with your superpowers, but it's a part of the plan or the process to get to where you want to go, ask for help. Reach out to your community and recruit a team of people to help you bring your dreams to life. Make a list of everything that needs to happen and highlight anything that hasn't been getting done. Maybe you consider releasing some of the more draining tasks on your to-do list, that aren't exactly in your wheelhouse, to another person who might be more equipped to accomplish them. For example, maybe you hire a virtual assistant or a professional cleaner for your household chores. You could also delegate tasks to yourself by scheduling them into your calendar. Set a reminder so that it gets done.

3. Detach: Spend a period away from your community. Especially if you're coming out of a busy season or a "summer" season. Do a digital detox and give yourself permission to go MIA while you get organized and take care of yourself. Let the Waning Moon serve as your reminder to physically detach from anything that's been weighing you down. Host a clothing exchange, have a yard sale, or donate anything that's been cluttering up your space. Give thanks for the old and welcome in the new. I love the symbolism of a tree shedding its leaves to preserve energy for the cold winter. Conserve your time and energy for what's most important to you. Use this season to organize and declutter, literally and symbolically. What do you want less of in your life? Let go of negative energy and release anything that's not serving you to make space for the blessings coming your way. Share anything that's been bothering you in your journal or with a therapist or a trusted friend to get it off your chest. Keep an open mind when you're setting goals and detach from any one specific outcome.

    As humans, we're constantly faced with difficult decisions. Remember that it's okay to say no if something doesn't align. During

Chapter 12

the Waning Moon phase, focus on personal responsibilities rather than tending to your community. We're social beings and we love to help, but as you receive invitations, don't hesitate to decline, especially if you're on the verge of burnout.

Trust your intuition.

Maybe you're invited to a family gathering. Maybe you're flattered by an opportunity to speak at an event. Maybe you're presented with a job offer and the money is good, but you're already at your wits end with work and you're starting to fall behind in other areas of life.

We love to serve, we love to give, and we really like to feel valued.

Maybe you worry about disappointing people, but if you're saying yes when you really mean no, you're not doing anybody a service. The most effective and sustainable way to help others is to honor your needs first, so that when the time comes, you have the utmost energy and love to give without spreading yourself thin.

If you know what's most important to you, your decisions will come easily. When you find yourself at a fork in the road, look to your core values for guidance.

What are your top three core values? Take a minute to think about it and write them down. Here are some examples: Love, service, freedom, fun, family, truth, beauty, peace, comfort, diversity, adventure, health, education, equality, accessibility, creativity, expansion, joy, sustainability.

When you're feeling overwhelmed by a growing to-do list, try writing down everything that you're doing monthly, then consider which tasks take priority and which might not be so important now. Maybe there's something that's urgent and it's important, so you do it right away. Maybe there's something that's important to you, but it's not urgent. Plan to do it as soon as possible by scheduling a date into your calendar. Maybe there's something that's urgent, but it's not that important to you or aligned with your gifts. This could be a task you might consider delegating. When you pinpoint items on your list that aren't urgent or important, you can choose to dump them all together or postpone them indefinitely.[21]

People can be really good at convincing us that something that's important to *them* is urgent, but in most cases, it's not. You don't have to drop everything and interrupt your life to respond in that very moment. I physically don't have the capacity to prioritize everyone else's priorities, and this doesn't make me a bad person. I'm a better version of myself when I'm honoring my needs and protecting my energy.

I live with my phone in Do Not Disturb mode and get back to messages and missed calls when I'm free to chat. (This also causes tension with my mom who likes to keep in touch all day long, but she's learned to respect my boundaries and knows not to freak out when I don't answer.)

In this 21st century world, we can reach friends and family across the globe thanks to the telephone and internet. We have access to unlimited information. Everything we could ever want to know can be found with the click of a button with a device that fits in the palm of our hand.

It's magical!

---

21. You can find a printable Action Priority worksheet inside of my Journaling Prompts for Joyful Living available at ShannonTheGoodWitch.com/TheHealthyHigh.

Chapter 12

But we must be intentional with this technological magic. It's powerful, and it's impacting us. It's shaping our thoughts and ideas. We must consciously choose who and what to let into our spaces, including news and media. Are you learning about topics that serve you or are you filling your mind with disempowering notions?

We can't control our circumstances, but we can control our thoughts. We get to choose who to follow and what to believe.

Just as it serves us to fill our minds with educational and inspirational materials, it serves us to seek silence and stillness so that we can hear Source speaking to us.

Get quiet and listen for the voice of your intuition. Let it come through!

In Chapter Nine: You are A Divine Creator, I shared some practices to help you quiet your mind and connect to your highest self. Revisit those anytime you need some ideas.

If you're like me and you tend to hyperfocus on tasks that aren't moving the needle forward, how can you release some of the distractions in your workspace? Maybe there's just one tiny closet or corner that you keep pleasantly pristine with things just the way you like them, so that you've got a place to go to ground down and tune in. If you don't have a space of your own like this, maybe you find a place in nature that you can visit to clear your head. Maybe you simply close your eyes and visualize a wide-open field.

Clearing Ritual for the Waning Moon:

Consider opening some windows and imagining fresh air flowing in to clear your space while any stagnant energy seeps outside. You could also close your eyes and visualize fresh air or smoke filling your space as you welcome peace and positivity into your field.

Here's a simple spell you can say to help you release any energy that doesn't belong to you:

North, South, East, West, clear this space, make it fresh.
When I rise, when I rest, in this space, I feel my best.

In Chapter Thirteen: Connect to your Divine Nature with the New Moon, I'll tell you why the New Moon Phase is the best time to kick off your work boots and take a vacation!

CHAPTER 13

Connect to Your Divine Nature with The New Moon

Figuratively speaking, the New Moon is a good time to fill your cup and recharge your batteries—To embrace the darkness and go inward to receive divine guidance from your soul so that you can set your intentions for the new lunar cycle with clarity.

When the world shut down in March 2020 and my calendar opened, I felt a sense of relief. I was stuck at home with couples calling left and right to cancel their events, just before the start of another busy wedding season. I saw other videographers and **wedding vendors feeling sad, panicked, and terrified about the state** of their businesses, so why was I celebrating? Soon enough, Alex and I were forced to postpone our own summer wedding, set for July 11, 2020, and I wasn't exactly happy about it, but I knew it would give me my time back and I felt even more relieved. Besides, we'd signed our marriage license a year earlier and I was already getting Alex's awesome benefits from his cushy accounting job, so really, there was no rush.

Quarantine blessed me with a sense of stillness I'd been craving, but the peace didn't last long. Spring was in the air and I'd been feeling restless, but not in the sense that I was bored or cooped up. It was more of an inspired feeling lacking direction. A couple of weeks into lockdown, I noticed a post about a group coaching course for female entrepreneurs. It captivated me in a way that I couldn't ignore. I was feeling lost in the midst of the uncertainty I was facing as a small business owner, and I knew I could use some clarity and accountability in my business strategy.

The post was from a woman named Danielle Langton, who I'd met a year earlier when her fiancé booked me to photograph his proposal. I had no idea she was running a program to empower women to start and scale their businesses, but when I stumbled across her page, I felt called to reach out. Her five-week course had already begun, but she assured me that it wasn't too late to sign up.

Right away, I felt good about my decision to invest in myself.

I joined the group and instantly felt energized, supported and hopeful for the future. I had a chance to take a closer look at the way I'd been managing my time, and as it turned out, I needed help. I used to journal and meditate daily, and I'd totally fallen out of the habit of reflecting. I was a hamster spinning on the wheel, just trying to keep up. I quickly realized that in the pursuit of building a profitable business, I'd lost sight of my core values and the reason that I started my own business in the first place—for freedom! I'd booked myself up so fully, that I was no longer making time to check in with my purpose.

But I think the real reason I hired Danielle was because I saw myself in her. I wanted to learn from her because I wanted to do

Chapter 13

what she was doing. I wanted to teach people how I'd found success in following my intuition, being resourceful, and using my natural gifts. I felt like an imposter, but I knew in my heart that I wanted to help people, and she was showing me that it was possible. Before I could do that though, I knew I had to get my own life and business in order. I was behind on my work, exhausted and had developed a bad habit of procrastinating. I needed some accountability and I fell in love with the coaching space. I loved connecting with like-minded, purpose driven women over our passions and creative pursuits.

I know it sounds like I'm about to share an uplifting story of how things finally turned around, but I hope you're not too disappointed to know that this is when things really started to go downhill.

Up until that point, I'd been figuring it out all on my own and learning from my mistakes along the way. I had stayed in my lane and always had clarity. Decision making came easily to me because I trusted my intuition.

Suddenly, I was looking outside of myself for guidance and to all these other women to tell me what to do next and found myself longing for a different life. I wanted a completely new business, but I was still using the time in our coaching sessions to figure out how to scale my existing one. Maybe a part of me thought that I *could* do it all and that I wouldn't have to let go of anything to start something new.

Either way, my thoughts and desires became intertwined with all the information I was consuming and the confusion flooded in.

But I dove in headfirst anyway and dedicated my spare time to launching a podcast and growing an email list while simultaneously purchasing a second home with Alex's help, renovating it and turning it into my photography studio. I'd also started renting out my new photobooth and picking up branding sessions to fill up all the extra time I had from the canceled weddings.

I took on some interns to assist me but training them turned out to be more work and didn't take any time-sucking tasks off my plate. I was hustling harder and wearing more hats than ever before. But I wanted to teach people everything I was learning—all these tools that I was using to change my life and "scale" my business.

The epiphany that I could be a coach and a teacher was a little ping from my intuition, and I see now that I was meant to learn this lesson—to experience so many teachable moments before I would make it here—but I was on the right path. I loved hosting a podcast, nurturing my email subscribers and showing up on social media, but I'd bitten off more work than I could chew.

Soon, quarantine lifted, weddings resumed, and socializing commenced. I was forced to show up, once again, in too many places. I had no choice but to put a pause on the podcasting and the blogging and all those things that were lighting me up because I hadn't carved out the systems to make it all sustainable. I was already missing family gatherings and friends' milestones because I had such a full plate. I felt guilty for documenting my own occasions when I had so many clients waiting on me to deliver their films and galleries, so I stopped carrying my camera unless I was on the clock.

By the end of the year, I felt sad, overwhelmed, unfulfilled and burned out again, but this time, I was almost completely out of money and at a loss for what to do next because I just couldn't stand the thought of taking on any more work. I felt like a terrible person for accepting new projects because I wanted to be available for my loved ones, but I had bills to pay, so I welcomed the clients with open arms. My inner world was caving in and on the outside, I was holding it all together with a pep in my step, saying yes to more projects and even more coffee dates, pretty much giving up any hope of ever getting out of the weeds.

Fast forward six months to August of 2021, after planning, replanning, and successfully throwing a kick-ass wedding for 250 guests then squeezing in a honeymoon road trip, I was spent. I'd just helped my mom move out of her deteriorating house and into a safe and comfortable apartment, and part of me was feeling relief from getting so many things checked off the to-do list, but there was still no end in sight to all the responsibilities I was managing.

I knew I had created the life I was walking around in, but I didn't want it anymore. I wished I could hand in my two weeks notice like I did five years earlier as a wide-eyed and bushy tailed twenty-three-year-old with infinite possibilities at her fingertips. But this wasn't the same. I had put my heart and soul into creating this business—into creating this life—so why was I feeling this way? I felt bad for losing the spark for my work. It was the first time in my life I'd ever really felt stuck.

I was at a crossroads, and I didn't know what to do.

Have you ever felt bound by your circumstances? Reflect back on a time you felt trapped or at a crossroads. What was it like? How did you break free? What did you learn? If you're feeling trapped now, please schedule a discovery call at ShannonTheGoodWitch.com/connect so that we can get you set up with the support you need to move forward.

That's when the tragic loss of our cat, Julie, ripped me open and helped me release all the emotions I'd been too busy to process. Through that experience, I found that breakdowns lead to breakthroughs and sometimes we have to hit rock bottom before we gain the strength to climb out of our holes and up the magic beanstalk. The thing to remember when you find yourself here is this: Don't try to fill the void.

Instead, explore it.

There's light to be found in even the darkest, deepest, shadowiest parts of yourself. The answers you seek are inside of you. So, if you're feeling stuck in the mud and you're not sure how to move forward, you're in a perfect place to begin the healing process. You might feel like Life is dragging you down, but it just wants you to get to the bottom of what's really bothering you so that you can learn and grow.

You don't have to wait for the next global pandemic to force you into quarantine or a life shattering crisis to give yourself permission to rest and recover. If you want to move mountains, you better rest up! Let the Dark Moon serve as your reminder to take a break, get some extra sleep, and plan rejuvenating activities that help you heal!

Here's a simple mantra you can say while the Moon is dark in the sky to remind you that you have everything you need within you to create a magical life:

New Moon Connection Spell

The Moon is dark, it hides above
I go within to find the love
To guide me toward what's good and true
What's best for me and best for you

Chapter 13

Three Actionable Steps You Can Take During the New Moon: A Symbolic Winter Season and a Time to Connect to Your Divine Nature

1. Dream: What could be more beneficial for your healing and personal development than rest? Utilize the period of darkness during a New Moon to relax and recover while the collective energy of the planet is at its lowest. It's important to stop and refuel before beginning a new project. You are worthy of down time! Give yourself permission to take a vacation or attend a yoga class or retreat where you can connect with your highest self more easily. Tenderly care for the temple you reside in so that you can fully experience the bliss of life through your human senses.

2. Download: Once you've created space to step away and reconnect with your intuition, you're bound to feel enlightened and full of inspired ideas. Keep a journal nearby for an easy place to store your downloads the moment they come through. I've come to realize that the same strategy works for my hopes and dreams. If there's ever a time to write something down, it's the moment when that light bulb goes off and I'm suddenly hit between the eyes with clarity. Inspiration is fleeting and the distractions of everyday life can quickly steal back your attention before you even realize that your intuition was speaking to you. So, when you find things that make you feel amazing, when you have an awesome idea or a vision for the future, write it down. Take note of it and make sure that you have a place to store your thoughts so that later when you're searching for some inspo, you have a place to look. This will look different for everybody. Maybe you use a word document or you record a voice memo to your phone.

3. Design: When that tiny little crescent appears in the sky after a few days of darkness, be reminded to carve out time for visualizing your dream life. As you imagine your future, don't filter yourself. Let your mind wander and explore all the different avenues. If you really want to have some fun with it, gather up some art supplies and colorfully bring your dream to life in the form of a vision board. Tap into your inner child, be creative and play! If you don't have the supplies to make a physical vision board, you could create a digital collage with Canva or Pinterest. You'll also want to practice visualizing your desires in your mind's eye. Tune into your senses and connect with the feelings you want to manifest in your life.

When and where do you get your best ideas? Are you in the shower? Are you on your morning run? Is it in the middle of the night? What's the easiest way for you to track those thoughts? A journal? Post-it notes? A Google Doc? A voice memo or a note on your phone? There are so many different ways that you can do it. Take a minute to think it through and come up with a strategy so that you're ready to capture inspiration the moment it strikes.[22]

After my "dark night of the soul," all the pent-up emotions I'd been hiding poured out of me in beautiful ways. I journaled and wrote poetry. I attend healing workshops and retreats that helped me share my experiences. I danced and enjoyed nature. I discovered new music and new ways to celebrate being alive. I focused on releasing trapped emotions and negative thought patterns. I changed my

---

22. Snag my Journaling Prompts for Joyful Living at ShannonTheGoodWitch.com/TheHealthyHigh to help with your visualization practice.

environment and stopped spending so much time in places and with people who weren't serving me. I found joy and fulfillment in my work again and cleared my calendar of any commitments that don't align with my values. I created simple routines in my daily life that support my unique human design and honor the ebbs and flows of my cyclical energy levels. I devoted sacred time and space to myself so that I could show up better able to serve the people around me. I stopped holding myself back by the weight of responsibilities that weren't mine to carry and I stopped trying to fix and control the people around me.

I started working on myself instead, realizing that **I am the only person responsible for my happiness.**

In Chapter Fourteen: Cultivate your Dream Life with the Waxing Moon, we'll get into the nitty-gritty of the final step of my lunar manifestation ritual, so don't stop now![23]

---

23. Head to ShannonTheGoodWitch.com/Moon for a list of supporting resources.

CHAPTER 14
Cultivate Your Dream Life with the Waxing Moon

In Chapter One: In the Weeds, we talked about a garden and the practice of planting the seeds of our greatest intentions and symbolically watering them until our gardens are rich with our favorite fruits and vegetables. By now, I have a feeling you're starting to gain a clearer vision of this abundant garden! But your garden isn't going to grow on its own. (Well, it might, but it will probably be overgrown with weeds and wildflowers.) Don't be afraid to dig in and get your hands dirty.

This part of the manifestation process isn't going to look perfect! Opposite of the Waning Moon Phase, that's great for cleaning up, clearing the way, and taking *aligned* action toward your *personal* goals, the Waxing Moon Phase is best for taking *inspired* action toward your *worldly* goals.

Imagine an artist painting a giant mural. She probably wears an apron and isn't afraid to make a big, beautiful mess with her painting supplies because she knows it will be worth the cleanup.

Learn from her and make a mess! You can clean up later.

When I finally committed to writing this book, I signed up for something called the "30 Day Book Writing Challenge" with Joshua Sprague.[24] I was told to write the entire rough draft without going back to edit anything until the entire draft was complete. Creating and editing use very different parts of our brain, so keep this in mind when you're making anything in life.

Allow your creative juices to flow freely and wildly! Who cares if you get messy? Does it really matter if you make a mistake? Don't let your fear of messing up stop you from showing up and giving it your best shot.

When I started my production company, I had no idea what I was doing. I didn't know how to run a business and I hardly knew how to use my camera, but I gave myself permission to learn on the go. I met up with a friendly Uber driver named Brandon McMillan who offered me free lessons and wound up with a new buddy to help me practice. I made it my mission to hire second shooters (like my new friend Brandon) that did know what they were doing, so that I could learn from them, while incorporating their high-quality shots into my wedding films. With every shoot, I improved. But I charged my worth from the very beginning and shared the wealth with my talented peers who helped me grow.

Way back when I stepped in front of the camera for my very first post-game interview with the head football coach after Duquesne beat Valparaiso at home on Rooney Field in 2011, do you think I felt confident? Hell no! Even after dozens of post-game

---

24. You can find a link to the 30 Day Book Writing Challenge at ShannonTheGoodWitch.com/TheHealthyHigh where you can also schedule a session with me to hash out the purpose for your book.

Chapter 14

interviews and hundreds of newscasts, my heart pounded every time I went live. But every single time I did something that scared me, I proved to myself that I could do anything!

If there's one thing you take away from this book, I hope it's this—**you add value to the world simply by existing.**

You will prosper by putting yourself out there and sharing your genius.

Don't be afraid to stand out or make a fool of yourself. If being yourself means being "weird," to hell with anyone who doesn't love you for you.

Not everyone is going to like you, but that's okay!

When you're true to yourself and express your creativity, you will attract people who love you and lift you up.

So, please, for goodness' sake, stop trying to fit in!

You are so needed! Whatever service that you're here to give, there is a demand for it. In his book, *Creating Affluence*, Dr. Deepak Choprah calls it "The Law of Demand and Supply." You were blessed with your unique experiences and perspectives for a divine reason. You're meant to share your story!

We all come from the same energetic source, yet each of us has chosen a particular soul, personality, body, upbringing, birthday, etc. to embody our unique thread of dharma. The purpose of living your dharma is beyond yourself. Yes, it will bring you abundance, but it will also uplift humanity.

We've all got something uniquely special to offer one another, and when we find something we love and that we're innately good at, we should share it with our communities. We're a part of something a whole lot bigger than ourselves. When we work together with the greater good in mind, we all win.

It doesn't matter where you come from or what you're starting out with. It's an even playing field and we've all got potential to make an impact. Have fun with the creative process and make something beautiful that only you can create!

What resources do you have available to you? How can you put them to good use? Gather up what you've got and get started!

Maybe you find that you've only got cucumber seeds, but you don't really like cucumbers. So, maybe you go to the local farmers market and trade another farmer for some tomato seeds. Yes of course, you could grow the cucumbers and trade those, but maybe you save yourself time and energy by planting the seeds of what you really wanted to grow from the get-go.

I hope you're not sick of all this gardening talk by now, but it's what keeps coming through for me and somehow, I bet, that even if you're not a master gardener, you get the picture.

The "dream life" you're creating is going to take nurturing, resourcefulness, and patience. Keep at it and before long, you'll be biting into a delectable meal made of fresh farm to table foods with plenty to go around. And you don't have to make every dish on your own to have a picnic! Do it potluck style and invite your guests to bring something they've made too. Share what you've got with the people around you and take a taste of everything they're offering!

"A dream you dream alone is only a dream. A dream you dream together is reality."

This is a John Lennon quote, but it reminds me of my soul sister, Ayfer Cicek, who says it in a beautiful Turkish accent. When I started classes for my coaching certificate, I was instructed to utilize the cohort Facebook group to find an accountability buddy. The first person I messaged had already found a partner who lived in the same state and kindly invited me in to make a three-person group, but I wished them well and continued my search. That's when I found Ayfer, a beautiful Middle Eastern woman holding a yoga pose in her photo. She was also late to the accountability party, so we teamed up. Worlds apart, we met bi-weekly for the next six months while we worked our way through the course from different time zones. Meeting Ayfer in the flesh was a miracle. She was from Istanbul and I was from Pittsburgh, so there were literally oceans between us, but we were magically brought together in Los Angeles.

That moment alone felt worthwhile of the $5,000 I'd invested in myself when I enrolled in the Dharma Coaching Institute seven months earlier. To have friends around the world with the same mission as me—what could be more powerful?

When I felt the pull to sign up for the program, I was low on funds after making the decision to stop booking weddings (the bread and butter of my business) so a $5,000 course should have seemed out of the question. Leading up to that point, I'd been looking forward to a slower summer, so I was surprised to find myself excited to commit to six hours a week of schoolwork. But my gut told me it was the right thing to do, so without hesitation, I opened a new credit card, made my payment and earned a bunch of reward points that later bought me a ticket to the city of angels where I'd meet Ayfer, Sahara Rose, Dr. Neeta Bushan, and one hundred more "Sun-Beings" at our graduation event![25]

---

25. Sahara Rose and Dr. Neeta Bushan are the co-founders of Dharma Coaching Institute. Both are best-selling author, and top-rated podcast hosts. You can find links to their books and some of my favorite podcast episodes at ShannonTheGoodWitch.com/TheHealthyHigh.

About a week after I enrolled, my dad sent me a check out of the blue. It was for $5,000—the same amount I paid for the program. He'd never really given me any money before that, so it was completely unexpected. He didn't know that I could use the money to help me pay for my education; he wanted me to invest it in some kind of stock or something, but in the end, he told me to do whatever I wanted with it. After that, he continued sending me checks sporadically.

Eventually, I found out that he'd gotten an inheritance from my Grandpa Dale and Grandma Eileen, so it felt as if they were looking out for me. I knew that I was on the right path, and they were on my side. But what I didn't appreciate enough was my dad. I mean I was grateful, but I see now that he had been my earthly angel all along.

Now, I'm a certified coach with a tribe of supportive friends all around the planet because I trusted my intuition and the Universe did its thing to sort out the details.

This is the power of manifestation at work! Follow the pings and the Universe will help you get to where you're going. I know you have angels too. So pay attention and act on the signs. Take that leap of faith and your spirit guides will be there to catch you and help you soar. Lead with your heart and you will go far.

What are you feeling inspired to create? Are you feeling excited about an upcoming project or opportunity? When could you schedule in time to get started?

When the moon is growing or "waxing," the collective energy of the planet is on the rise. Lean in and take inspired action while you've got the support of the magical moon on your side!

Here's a simple spell I use to help me cultivate more power during the Waxing Moon:

Waxing Moon Power Spell

The moon is growing in the sky
My magic powers are on the rise

Three Actionable Steps for the Waxing Moon Phase: A Symbolic Spring Season and a Time to Cultivate Your Dream Life

1. Decide: At some point, you've got to commit to a goal and choose a path forward. Announce your intentions to the people in your community for support and accountability. Tell them what you're up to! You've committed to your next move and that's a reason itself to celebrate. Shout it from the rooftops! If it's freedom you want— focus on that! If it's love you want— focus on that! If it's adventure you want—focus on that! Decide that it's yours and make an unchangeable decision to go for it. You don't need a plan, just a definite purpose, and anything you want will be yours if you keep at it until you succeed.

2. Devote: So, your boots are strapped and you've decided on a trail, but what's going to keep you going when the hills gets rocky and muddy? Having a clear purpose behind your goals will fuel you forward with energy and passion for your pursuits. Know your mission and keep it at the forefront of every decision you make. Figure out who you're going to help and how you're going to make a positive impact. Follow through on the promises you've made and show up for yourself like you'd show up for someone else.

3. Do the work: I like to think of this part of the ritual as the "sacred doing." At some point, you've got to get up out of your meditation seat and take the necessary steps to bring your visions to life. Think of your purpose as you water the seeds of your greatest intentions and you will experience tremendous growth. Don't let a fear of messing up or making mistakes hold you back from showing up! You don't have to be perfect to make progress. There's always going to be a chance to refine or change course, but how will you ever figure out what's working and what's not if you don't act?

Let the moon serve as your daily reminder to honor the ebbs and flows of your energy levels. Use it to assist you in your manifestation practice, but don't worry about aligning your life perfectly with the lunar calendar. This simple ritual is only intended to help you understand your cyclical nature.[26]

Harness it if you dare!

In the final chapter, I'll share some tips for manifesting money, because I think we could all benefit from a little more of that kind of magic in our lives. There are infinite ways to welcome more wealth into your life, and I'm here to show you that it's easier than you think.

If you'd like to work less so that you can live more, keep reading!

---

[26]. In exchange for your email, I'll send you a free Lunar Planner. You can find it at ShannonTheGoodWitch.com/Moon.

CHAPTER 15
Manifesting Money

In coaching sessions with my clients, I often notice that money is the biggest obstacle standing in their way of acting toward their wildest dreams and life goals. Sometimes they feel trapped in a time sucking job they hate because it's paying the bills. Sometimes they don't believe that they can make any money using their gifts or doing things they love, so they put their passions on hold while they save up for retirement. Sometimes, they're not even sure how much they're earning or spending monthly, so they just keep making do with what they have. They find themselves in the same dilemma, time and time again, wondering why all their money seems to magically disappear when they need it.

Money certainly isn't the end all be all to happiness, but it certainly makes life easier—it opens doors and helps us get to where we're going! Money allowed me to publish this book with the help of a team of seasoned professionals. Thanks to my coaches, editors and designers at *Big Idea to Best Seller,* I could focus on creative writing and let the experts handle the details of getting my story out into the world with a bang. After all, my goal wasn't just to write a book, it was to publish a bestseller!

Money is always available—just like magic is—but we must be open to it!

And maybe you're thinking,

"Of course I'm open to receiving money! Give me all the money!"

Unfortunately, I could argue that those words you're hearing in your head are coming from your *conscious* mind, but it's your *subconscious* mind that's ruling your life. So, if you want your power back, you're going to have to change your mind on a subconscious level!

Maybe you ignore your money because you feel like you don't understand it. It's possible you grew up like my husband, believing that you had to work hard, get a traditional job to earn an income, and settle for a less than extraordinary life because you're not special enough to make it in the big leagues and security is worth more than fulfillment.

But I promise, you are worthy, capable and deserving of having it all.

What beliefs do you carry around money? Think about your authority figures and what they said about money growing up. Write down anything that's coming through.

Money is energy, just like you and me. All you need to do is tune into its frequency. Get its attention! Wave it down and show it that you've got a purpose for it. Clear any physical or energetic blocks and soon, you'll be ready to receive.

Chapter 15

Your most profound and inspired ideas are going to come through when your mind isn't so busy stressing about paying your bills, saving up enough to take a desperately needed vacation, or showing up again at a job that you hate.

You deserve to be financially free without being time bound!

You are a timeless spiritual being in mortal human form. If you're lucky, you've got about eighty years on earth. Don't waste it worrying. Life is meant to be enjoyed!

Why would you let your fear stand in the way of your freedom?

If looking at your bank account scares you, clear your belief that money is scary by doing a little research and planning. Open your mind to all the possibilities and invite experts into your life to help. Meet with an advisor to make sure you're set for success. Enroll in automated payments so that you're not stressing over late fees or silly subscriptions that you don't use.

Pay attention to how you speak about your finances and try to shift any negative language. Focus on the abundance already present in your life and talk about that! Consciously focus on all the good you could do with the money you're calling in and do the best you can with what you already have. Repeat the mantra,

"Money in my hands makes the world a better place" until you believe it and don't wait until you're wealthy to start being charitable. Find ways that you can volunteer your time and energy to the causes you support. There, you'll find like-minded people who will lift you up!

If you could make anything of your life over the next five years, and money or time were unlimited, what would you create? What do you

see for your career, relationships, finances, health, home, spirituality, and overall sense of happiness and wellbeing? Think about all the pillars of your life and be specific.

When I started Shannon Chavez Production back in 2016 as a confident, carefree, twenty-three-year-old with a zest for life and a passion for art and service, my business grew organically with little planning or strategy involved. I simply opened myself up to clients and believed that I was good enough to serve them. I didn't know everything, but I didn't let that stop me. I learned on the go and trusted in my capacity to solve problems and overcome challenges along the way. Success came easily to me because I believed I was worthy, and I wasn't afraid to fail or admit that I was far from an expert in my field. I took pride in my savvy ability to make money helping people in a way that felt fun and allowed me to be creative. I didn't know everything, but I enlisted help and figured things out on the go.

I wanted to show my peers that if I could do it, they could too!

My ambition paired with an ability to stay open and present to the opportunities that presented themselves got me far, but before I knew it, I was suffocating beneath a pile of work with no end in sight. Although I loved my clients and I loved my business, I'd run myself dry and needed to get organized and create systems to help me catch up.

Heading into 2022, I raised my prices and committed to wrapping up the projects that were already on my calendar. I gave myself permission to say no to any new invitations that flowed in and devoted my energy to my own personal dharma discovery. When I signed up for Dharma Coaching Institute that spring, I

Chapter 15

developed a routine around my weekly calls and coaching pods and looked forward to waking up early to complete the training modules.

Through my dharma studies, I realized that I was running my production company using the *skills* I'd developed through years of practice, rather than using my *superpowers*. Photography and filmmaking were mediums I'd mastered to help me document the magic that I have a natural ability to see in people and in the world around me. I loved sharing this magic with my clients and it gave me a means to earn a living, but all the moving parts and technical stuff I had to manage before I could deliver a project were burning me out.

When I wrapped up those weddings and graduated with my coaching certifications in October 2022, Alex and I prepared our house for renters and left Pittsburgh at the start of 2023 for ten weeks of travel. During a month in Hawaii, I created a digital course called *The Good Life Masterclass* and published it for free so that I could share all I'd learned about purpose and manifestation with people around the world without burning out again. I'd finally reached a slower pace of life, and I was afraid to lose it.

To protect me, my subconscious mind formed a belief that money equaled burnout. I'd fallen so deeply in love with the simple pleasures in life that my ambition and desire for any form of material wealth fell to the back burner.

Deep down, I didn't want my new coaching business to succeed because that might mean I'd burn out again.

It's said that with great power comes great responsibility. That notion used to scare the crap out of me! For a little while, this belief served me well. It helped me to make room in my life for rest and self-care, but it was keeping me from my potential. I even started giving away my services for free. I was afraid that charging for my work meant that I'd have to go above and beyond and burn myself out in the process.

That's when a funny thing happened: I realized that I was going above and beyond whether people paid me or not. It was simply in my nature to give!

Once I realized that I did have the capacity to handle more responsibility and that I wanted to keep serving with my whole heart, I understood that my sustainable success depended on charging my worth. So I started charging for my coaching services, opened myself up to brand photography clients, and abolished the insane belief that money equaled burnout.

If you're wondering how to manifest more money so that you can stop hustling and start thriving, use the same steps I've already mapped out in my lunar manifestation ritual.

1. CELEBRATE the abundance already present in your life and dig into your existing resources. Build a habit of checking in on your finances consistently and do your best to make the most of the money you've got. Get really clear about what's coming in and what's going out each lunar cycle. Maybe you make a ritual of it with your favorite moon marker. Get excited about your purchases and give thanks for any stream of money already flowing into your life. Honor where you're starting out.
2. CLEAR the way for abundance to flow in by releasing energetic blocks or limiting beliefs. There's more than enough money available to you to cover everything you could ever possibly want or desire. Consider making room

for a new paid opportunity to come along or for a business idea to blossom. Create space in your day to day for new money-making opportunities that feel aligned. Hire a helper in your business or buy a new asset to increase income and get the tax write-off. Sell anything you don't need and consider letting go of expenses that aren't serving you. Clear up any outstanding debts that are costing you interest or stressing you out, and if you need help, relinquish the **responsibility of managing your finances to an expert or trusted mentor.** [27]

3. **CONNECT** to your purpose for the money you're calling in and get clear on your plans for it. Tune into the version of you who already has everything they desire. What are you doing? Who are you helping? How does it feel? What amount of money do you need to sustain that lifestyle? It's all possible! **Getting specific in the numbers will only aid in your subconscious mind's ability to seek out the money where it's eagerly waiting for you to find it. Plus, you might find that you're already closer to your goals than you think!**

4. **CULTIVATE** money by nurturing your existing finances, just like you would nurture a relationship with a person you love. The more you pay attention to your money, the **more it will grow. Give it some tender loving care and find** joy in the process. Keep it somewhere safe like in a high interest savings account so that you earn a little extra just for saving. Focus on growing a cushion of about six months of expenses, so that you can confidently shift your focus

---

27. Visit ShannonTheGoodWitch.com/manifestingmoney for supporting resources.

to making investments in yourself. Set clear goals for your long- and short-term future based on the vision of your highest self and the dream life you're calling in. Water the seeds of your intentions by devoting your time, money, and energy to what matters most to you.

Look to this acronym for some extra guidance when you're manifesting money:

Creating S.P.A.C.E. for Money to Flow

Safety. Purpose. Accessibility. Community. Expansion.

Safety: Money wants to feel safe and supported. When we're living in survival mode, our thoughts are focused on keeping us alive. Our brains still think we're being hunted or that there's a scarcity of food. This keeps us acting on our primal instincts rather than from our higher brain. How can you create a sense of safety in your life? Maybe this is through working with a therapist to reprogram your subconscious mind. Perhaps you simply create a safe space where your body feels relaxed and at ease while you check your bank statements and bills. When you're stressed about money or your career or what you're going to eat for dinner, you're feeding into that survival brain and telling your body that it needs to heighten its senses. It will start working overtime out of fear. Schedule in some **time to organize your finances and create a budget. Get comfortable** with checking your accounts on a routine basis and ask for help when you need it.

Chapter 15

Purpose: Money is energy and energy must flow to grow! Money wants to know that you've got plans for it! What are you going to do with it? Maybe there's a person or an organization that you're going to help. Maybe you want to send your kids to college or buy your parents a house. Maybe you want to take your spouse on a romantic vacation to relight the spark in your marriage. Maybe you want a breast reduction to solve your lifelong struggle with back pain. Maybe you want to start a charity that's going to help people find permanent housing. Get to the bottom of whatever it is you want and keep it front of mind. Your subconscious mind is a problem solver. If you give it an assignment, it will seek out solutions. Focus on the exact amount of money you need to bring your visions to life. Don't worry about how you're going to get the money. Just make plans for it, talk about what you're going to do with it, and act as if you know it's on its way!

Accessibility: Give money a means to get to you! Maybe you start a new business and order a square card reader. You wouldn't have a brick and mortar without a cash register, would you? (Well, maybe you would, but you'd probably accept Apple Pay!) Make it easy for people to pay you and don't be afraid to fork over your bank account numbers online. Direct deposit is the way to go! When I started accepting credit cards rather than forcing my clients to write me a check or meet me with cash, I lessened the resistance and booked more projects on the spot. Create a system that allows you to receive money on command. For example, you could share your Venmo QR code. Maybe you create a simple digital product that you sell through your website. Perhaps you set up a GoFundMe account or an Instagram fundraiser. There are a million and one possibilities in this modern day, technology-friendly world! It's becoming easier and easier to receive money instantly.

Community: Add value to your community. People are going to be willing to repay the favor someday. They're going to want to donate to your cause or pay for your service because they already know, like and trust you. Maybe they even nominate you for an award or help you apply for a scholarship. Maybe they'd be willing to invest in you! Lean into your community and offer yourself as an asset.

Expansion: The biggest game changer for me when it came to manifesting money was when I focused on expansion. Why keep yourself small when it comes to your financial goals? Invite as much wealth as you desire into your life and create space for it to flow! This is a perfect place for me to mention that sometimes, less is more. Don't be afraid to release streams of income that no longer feel aligned so that you can free up energy for something better. Keep your purpose in mind as you open to expansive opportunities.

If you want more money, you've got to start asking for it. Craft an invitation. Consciously welcome it into your life by calling it in.

I used to invite wealth into my life by visualizing checks in the mail. When my wedding business was thriving, I'd collect my checks and play with them like monopoly money! I constantly had checks arriving in the mail from my clients. Eventually, I started visualizing direct deposits into my bank account! Now, I get pinged every **single day with money flowing in. Together, Alex and I have sixteen streams of income and counting. You can create openings like this for money to flow to you too and there are so many ways that you can do it!**

Chapter 15

You could say a simple prayer to the Universe or visualize checks coming in the mail like I did, but if you want to speed up the results, you can literally ask a person or entity to give you money; this doesn't mean to ask for a handout, even though you totally could—people love to help! Sometimes it looks like sending a proposal, applying for a grant, or asking for a job. Sometimes it looks like taking out a loan or opening a credit card that offers a sign-on bonus. Sometimes it looks like selling some furniture that you own or a piece of art that you painted. Maybe you rent out your car or a room in your house. Maybe you shovel your neighbor's sidewalk or offer to walk their dog. Maybe you throw a party and charge a cover. You could create some kind of tangible offer such as a digital course or a book on your favorite topic. Once it's published, you can relax and enjoy your life while the money pours in.

Brainstorm five ways that you could invite more money into your life. Write them down and circle one that you're going to act on this week!

Money is always going to be available to you, and there's more than enough to go around! Invite it in, give it a purpose, create a means to receive it and you will have a new sustainable way to manifest money without ever burning out again. It's going to take a little bit of effort up front, but soon, money will flow into your bank account while you're sleeping, while you're traveling, and while you're living your best life.

Before you go, I've gathered a few final sentiments in the coming pages that I'd love for you to take away. You're crazy close to the end, so hang around just a tiny bit longer if you want to make all that you've learned here sustainable!

CONCLUSION
Before You Go

"You must first have the knowledge of your power, second the courage to dare, and third, the faith to do."
—Charles Haanel, *The Master Key System*

You are creating the world around you.

If you didn't know that before picking up this book, I'm glad that you know now. If this news felt alarming to you as you thought about your current circumstances and you worried,

"Oh my gosh, did I really manifest this? How could I have created this?"

Don't stress! Now that you're aware of your power, you can start to shift your attention toward your heart's desires.

If you had a magic wand, what would you create for your life? What change would you make in the world around you? What impact would you make in your community? Visualize a reality where

all your desires are easily met. What does it feel like? How does it look?

Essentially, you do have a magic wand. You are more in control than you might think. But if right now, you're not sure what you would create, you're not alone. Maybe you've been so caught up in the chaos of life that you've forgotten what matters to you. But what if you made time to remember?

What was the potential you saw in yourself when you picked up this book? What did you believe was possible?

Come back to *The Healthy High* anytime you need a reminder of the magical being you are inside. Get crystal clear about what it is that you want so that you can start to ask for it. The Universe isn't going to give you what you want unless it knows what you want. You aren't going to know what you want if you don't make the time to ask.

What are your life goals? Take a moment to write down three to five things you'd be proud to accomplish in this lifetime and why.

You are going to have to put in some effort to cultivate your dream life, but it shouldn't feel hard. It should feel fulfilling, energizing, and inspired. When you make the time to nurture yourself, you will be able to give more and make an even bigger impact than you're already making. Take it day by day and for goodness' sake, rest when you're tired. The sun will rise and you will begin again.

Your days make up your life. If you want a grand life, fill it with grand days. Take a moment

to visualize your perfect day from start to finish and don't hold back. Dream big, get creative, and have fun with it. What does it look like? How does it feel?

If you've made it here, I hope you're feeling inspired. Maybe a newfound sense of purpose has jolted you out of your seat and just like that, you're off to the races. But before you saddle up and ride off into the sunset, I wanted to pass along a small bag I've packed up with a few more tokens of practical magic to sustain you through your adventure. Remember, you're talking to a fellow action-taker here; I can't read your mind, but I have walked in your boots.

If you're anything like I used to be, you're already setting goals and making big moves. You're amped up and motivated. You're probably itching to gallop away toward your greatest aspirations.

But how will you feel in a few days when Life steals back your attention?

You're a multi-dimensional, creative being with divine callings that can give you wings. I'd love to imagine that this book has helped you lift off toward the stars, but I know what it's like for everyday responsibilities to pull you back to reality.

So, when gravity weighs in, close your eyes and visualize your highest self. What would they do in this situation?

Who is the version of you that's already living the dream? Don't limit your mind to what you currently believe is possible for you. Get creative and lay it all out on the table.

In Chapter Nine: You are a Divine Creator, I shared four simple steps to manifesting anything.

Here they are again:

1. Acknowledge your power.
2. Ask for what you want.
3. Act as if it's coming.
4. Appreciate whatever comes.

Those are the steps in simple terms, but now that you've got a deeper grasp on manifestation, I'll serve it up in a less tangible format, but one I'm sure you've got the capacity to understand.

The four fundamentals to manifestation are as follows:

1. Connect: Tune into the feelings of your heart's true desire through meditation, journaling or any creative activities that help you enter a flow state where you can be guided by your highest self
2. Visualize: Get clear on what you want and how you want it to feel. Be specific when you're putting in your request to the Universe. Oprah Winfrey says "Create the highest grandest vision possible for yourself because you become what you believe."
3. Embody: Be the version of yourself that already has everything you desire! Embody the qualities of your truest, fullest expression and begin to act as though you have already received everything you're calling in. Do whatever you can to raise your vibration and use that energy you've cultivated to take aligned action toward your dreams.
4. Surrender: Follow your intuition and act on inspiration. Trust your gut and do what feels right. Be present and be open to the opportunities presenting themselves at every

Conclusion

moment. This final step requires patience and an unwavering faith in the divine organizing power of the Universe! Remember that everything happening now is leading you to the fulfillment of your desires.

The more you can deepen your connection to the version of yourself that you aspire to be, the easier it will become to embody the actions of that person and live out your potential. Try not to let your old identity stand in the way of the "who" you're becoming, but don't lose sight of who you are now. I guarantee you're further along than you think, so give yourself credit for making it this far.

Becoming who you're meant to be and manifesting the life you desire begins with knowing, loving, and trusting who you already are.

Be true to yourself and the rest will fall into place.

If there's something you're working to change in your life, don't quit as soon as you fall off the horse. Learn from the fall and hop back up with compassion and pride in your ability to shake it off and try again. Keep growing and above all else, never give up. If you want to get from point A to point Z, it might be a long road ahead. Pace yourself, enjoy the journey, and let the moon remind you that in every ending, there's a new beginning.

I'll be right here, cheering you on along the way.

I'm eternally grateful that you've accompanied me on this quest for self-discovery. Please keep in touch by following along on Instagram at @ShannonTheGoodWitch. Send me a message and let me know what you're up to. I can't wait to see what you manifest! If you'd be so kind as to leave a review of this book on Amazon, send me a screenshot or post it to your stories and tag me. I'd love to share your thoughts with my audience. Thanks a million for being a part of my story.[28]

---

[28]. Visit ShannonTheGoodWitch.com/services for a list of my current coaching offers so that we can move forward together and don't forget to join my email list so that we can stay in touch!

FAREWELL POEM:
When the Spring Comes

May you blow where the wind takes you
and land in new and fruitful soil.
May you sink into the depths of the earth and lay restfully
as the ground freezes above your sleepy eyes.
May you take the winter to be silent—
To be still.
And when the spring comes and the birds return,
may you awaken with a full soul and ready heart
to leap up and blossom into the perfect being
you are certain to become.
May the sweet simple joys in life
satisfy and sustain you.
May the sights and sounds of nature
serenade you softly.
And may serenity shadow you through every cyclical season,
until the end of time.

ACKNOWLEDGEMENTS

Thank you, Jake Kelfer and the entire *Big Idea to Best Seller* team for making my self-publishing journey easy and enjoyable, especially Mikey Kershisnik, Adrienne Dyer, and Ashton Renshaw.

Thank you, Joshua Sprague for creating the *30 Day Book Writing Challenge*—Knowing there would be an email from you, waiting in my inbox each morning, had me jumping out of bed to write!

Thank you, Clarise Fearn for gifting the world your creativity and capturing the essence of this book in a painting for the front cover! Your vibrant energy shines through in all you do!

Thank you to my strong, beautiful, independent Mumma, Patricia Chavez, for blessing me with the most magical life and teaching me how to dance—You are my hero. I wouldn't be here if you hadn't manifested me. I love you beyond measure!

Thank you to my late father, Steven Chavez, for your authenticity, carefreeness and generosity—You are my angel. I wouldn't be me without you.

The Healthy High

Thank you, Alex Olon, my life partner and best friend, for encouraging me to share our story. In loving you, and in being loved by you, I found myself. You bring out the best in me and give me the confidence to shoot for the starts. Together—and with a good night's sleep—we can do anything!

Thank you, Longfellow Sonnie Jim, for grounding me in the place that I'd finally finish this book and thank you, sweet Julie girl, for showing me what I needed to see.

Thank you to the 22-year-old girl who opened her heart and started wiring this book in 2015.

Thank you to me, the 31-year-old woman who decided to finish what she started all those years ago. I'm proud of you for clearing space in your days to pursue your callings.

Thank you, God, for your eternal love and support.

Thank you, Spirit Guides, for leading me here.

Thank you, dear Moon, for healing me.

And finally, thank YOU, my beloved reader, for walking this path with me—I'm honored and oh so grateful to be your cheerleader! You will never have to go it alone.

AUTHOR BIO

Shannon Chavez, also known as "Shannon~The Good Witch" is a Spiritual Life Coach and Soul Purpose Coach, certified through the Dharma Coaching Institute in 2022. After abandoning her career in television news in 2016 with a desire for more fulfillment in her life and work, she manifested her own production company as a photographer and filmmaker—two skills she still proudly uses today as a Brand Photographer and creative entrepreneur. During a spiritual awakening in 2021, Shannon devoted her life to becoming the highest version of herself so that she could help others do the same. Through coaching, books, and digital products, Shannon teaches her practical approach to dharma and manifestation with a mission to empower all people to live their purpose and fulfill their desires without burning out. She wrote *The Healthy High*, to help overwhelmed, multi-passionate, visionaries create space in their lives for what's *most* important to them, so that they can stop hustling and start living! Shannon has a passion for service and a love for magic and nature. You can usually find her writing, dancing, or hosting a gathering. She wanders the world with her life-partner, Alex, chasing sunsets and collecting experiences to share with her community. Follow along with her adventures at @ShannonTheGoodWitch on Instagram and visit ShannonTheGoodWitch.com to learn more about her current offers.

Made in the USA
Middletown, DE
18 June 2024

55608764R00123